To my dear late friend, Robert Milne, and so many happy memories.

Roger Geoffrey Carlund

JACARANDA, MR JAMES

AUSTIN MACAULEY PUBLISHERS™

LONDON • CAMBRIDGE • NEW YORK • SHARJAH

A CIP catalogue record for this title is available from the British Library.

ISBN 9781398466388 (Paperback)
ISBN 9781398466395 (ePub e-book)

www.austinmacauley.com

First Published 2022
Austin Macauley Publishers Ltd®
1 Canada Square
Canary Wharf
London
E14 5AA

My thanks to the media centre, Aberdeen Central Library, for their PC, printing and photocopying facilities, which enabled me to produce *Jacaranda, Mr James* for publication. The ever-helpful staff was always there, if IT help was required.

Table of Contents

The Blue Jacaranda

Jacaranda mimosifolia is a subtropical, fern-like deciduous tree, of the Bignoniaceae family, native to South America (Argentina, Bolivia and most likely Brazil).

It is commonly known as jacaranda or blue jacaranda.

Many of these trees can also be seen on the subtropical Portuguese island of Madeira, in the Atlantic Ocean. In sea-level villages, they enjoy the temperatures needed to bloom. They are also a striking feature in the centre of the island's capital, Funchal, where they can be seen along the sloping Avenida Do Infante, leading on to Avenida Arriaga, past, *Cafe Ritz, Blandy's Wine Lodge, The Golden Gate* restaurant and near *Cafe Apolo*, by Se Cathedral.

The long-lasting purple-blue flowers bloom in April and are present before the fresh, new green leaves appear.

The jacaranda trees put on a spectacular display in spring, when the beautiful, lightly fragrant, trumpet-shaped flowers cover the trees with bloom, and form vivid pools of purple-blue on the ground, as they fall.

****

List of Songs Featured
(In Order of Text):

1. *La Bamba* – Los Lobos (p28, 75)
2. *Half A Minute* – Matt Bianco (p28)
3. *The Girl from Ipanema* – Astrud Gilberto (p29)
4. *Let's Face the Music and Dance* – Nat King Cole (p31)
5. *Cavatina* – John Williams (p37)
6. *Happy* – Pharrell Williams (p44, 73, 88)
7. *Senorita* – Shawn Mendes, Camila Cabello (p74)
8. *We Have All the Time in The World* – Louis Armstrong (p83)
9. *Time To Say Goodbye* – Instrumental orchestra (pl23)
10. *Love Is in The Air* – John Paul Young (pl25)

Numbers 1, 2, 3, 6, 7, and 10 are sung live, by vocalists at, *Hole in One* bar/restaurant.

Number 5 is played outdoors live, in the cafe centre of Funchal.

Number 8 is played 'in James' head', as he strolls along the Promenade.

Number 4 is played 'in James' dream'.

Number 9 is background/piped instrumental music at, *Le Jardin* restaurant.

****

Chapter 1
Towards Funchal

He could see the Atlantic Ocean below, sufficiently close to make out the wave patterns and the occasional ship. The plane was gradually losing height, as it bypassed over the small tourist island of Porto Santo, to the northeast–known for its golden beach, its small town of Vila Baleira, a hotel or two and its connection to Christopher Columbus. James poured the remains of his second Chilean Merlot into his plastic glass and handed the small bottle to the passing steward. Continuing to the southeast, the plane bypassed over the llhas Desertas, the uninhabited smaller, narrow islands, home only to a few goats and rabbits but also to large, black poisonous spiders.

As the high mountainous terrain, crags and cliffs came into view, James felt the customary tingle down his spine as through his fellow-passengers' window, he saw the familiar panorama of terracotta roofs on the hillsides of the subtropical island of Madeira.

He could hear the hum of quiet chatter from nearby seats. As he knew, the airport and its previous very short runway had both been enlarged in recent years. Prior to that, James had most definitely seen some passengers pray before landing and take-off, when the plane mercifully rose upwards as opposed to plunging into the Atlantic. Now, a slightly lengthened runway came into view, as the plane swung around for its gradual, slow descent to the airport at Santa Cruz, on the southeast coast of the island. As it safely touched down, a polite ripple of applause filtered along the aisle.

After a short taxi journey to its stopping point near to the airport's entrance, all passengers disembarked, greeted by the warm, light breeze and were escorted on foot by airport personnel dressed in yellow jackets. Other stopping points required a short journey by airport coach, to safely transfer passengers on arrival and departure.

With the formalities of Passport Control and Baggage Reclaim over, James proceeded through to the meeting point for inter-island transfers. He made his way towards the numerous tour company personnel holding up signs with the different names of different arrivals. It didn't take James long to spot his name, 'Mr Harris'. The driver handed him an envelope, with the usual details for his welcome, took his large, olive-green suitcase and led the way out of the terminal, to the area for private transfers.

They passed the line of waiting yellow taxis and crossed the narrow road. As he made to take his seat behind the driver, James looked over the top of the car to the expanse of the Atlantic. It was late afternoon and the sky above was a vivid, clear blue. With his suitcase safely in the boot and his travel bag on his lap, he watched the driver place his key in the ignition and start the car's engine. "Pestana Miramar?" the driver asked, looking ahead through the windscreen.

"Por favor, please," James replied. The black saloon slowly made its way out of the airport area and onto the motorway. The route ahead would include passing through various hillside tunnels—a masterpiece of Portuguese engineering—and lead James towards Madeira's capital, the small city of contrasts, culture and colours, the city of Funchal.

Chapter 2
Mr James Returns

The car was travelling at a steady speed, having driven through some hillside tunnels, before coming to a bend on a further stretch of open motorway. This presented James with a stunning view of Funchal, the port and the Atlantic Ocean. Below to the left was the town centre and above to the right was the hillside panorama. He always anticipated these views during the earlier part of the journey and they never ceased to take his breath away.

Turning off the motorway, the driver took the car down the various streets leading towards James' destination. Stopping at traffic lights, he looked left and saw the enormous, Savoy *Palace Hotel*, which dominated the view of the ocean. He would walk along one evening and take a lift up to the fourteenth floor Roof Bar, for a beer, a seat by the infinity pool, and the night-time views.

They turned right onto the main road, Estrada Monumental. Farther ahead to the left, James looked across to, *Reid's Palace Hotel*, in its pink glory. Nearer to the right, the car slowed, turned and drove through the gates of Pestana Miramar, where James' small apartment would be his home for the next two weeks. The car gently bumped over the cobbled incline, turned left, past the huge central palm tree, surrounded by a small island of subtropical plants and flowers, and stopped. James thanked the driver, gave an appropriate tip and carried his suitcase and shoulder bag up the ramp, towards the entrance to Reception. After waiting for a few minutes, while a young couple made polite enquiries about departure times, he approached the marble-topped desk, parked his luggage and presented his passport. The ever-pleasant, ever-efficient Ricardo looked up from his screen and smiled at him. "Welcome back, Mr James."

Chapter 3
Settling In

He opened up the sliding glass door to his balcony and stepped outside. On three floors and the penthouses above, the crescent of apartments had been designed with traditional features, including terracotta roofs at the top. A semicircle of tall palms overlooked the pool below and some apartment balconies were framed on both sides by virtual waterfalls of bougainvillaea. James considered his balcony to be the best one for a show of these splendid flowers. Indeed, he would sometimes on return from his daily excursions, walk past the pool and at a short distance, look up to his first-floor apartment and say quietly to himself, "Yes, James, definitely the best apartment for bougainvillaea."

The separate, refurbished old hotel was situated near the pool, also overlooking the palms and lush, subtropical plants. On the other side of the hotel, guests overlooked the thoroughfare of Estrada Monumental and the Atlantic beyond.

From the left of his balcony, James could see two large cruise ships berthed at the port and farther along, he saw the Porto Santo ferry at its moorings. He went inside, closed the balcony door and looked at his well-appointed studio apartment, tastefully furnished and decorated in traditional wood and ceramic tiles. As always, he unpacked and hung up his two dress jackets, his leather blouson jacket, trousers, shirts, two waistcoats and travel bag in the wardrobe, placing his shoes beneath. Other items he stored in the chest of drawers. He transferred his daily toiletries onto a shelf in the shower room. He secured his passport, travel documents, currency, camera and cufflinks in the wardrobe safe. He checked the small kitchen for the usual stock of washing-up liquid, all-purpose cloth, pot scrubber, tea towel and condiments. He looked in the large mirror opposite his bed, combed his hair, locked his door and took the lift up to the roof terrace and the upper pool. He made his way to the Pool Bar, which was overlooked by the adjoining well-landscaped apartments of the Pestana Village. As he approached the bar, he was pleased to see the familiar smiling face of Miguel. "Welcome back, Mr James. Como esta? How are you?"

"Fine thank you, Bem obrigado, Miguel. It is always good to be back." Miguel was already pouring a large Coral beer. He placed it on the marble bar, in front of James, who took it over to a nearby table, the one he always chose, if it was available, for a touch of the late afternoon sun. As usual, he paid cash at Miramar, Miguel having tucked the bill inside a drinks menu on the table. Now, James could sit back and relax. He was 'in situ', far from home on this subtropical island, but very much at home.

Chapter 4
The Winter Garden

After his customary beer on arrival, he made the short walk to the nearer of the two local mini-markets. James loaded his basket with essential supplies for his apartment: buffet breakfast items, water, fresh mango juice, milk, coffee, beers, Portuguese white wine—for the late afternoon balcony sun—black olives, pistachio nuts and napkins.

On his return to the apartment, he remembered to avoid the sprays on each side of the driveway, which rotated slowly, to water the exotic plants and flowers in the late afternoon. His shopping appropriately stored, he decided to sit on the balcony for a short while and plan his evening: no change of clothes, only a quick freshen up and his leather blouson jacket. At seven-thirty at Reception, he'd order his usual taxi for eight-fifteen, then take the lift to the Winter Garden bar for a large beer, to whet his appetite for the evening ahead.

The circular, high-ceilinged Winter Garden was tastefully furnished with cushioned wicker chairs, glass coffee tables and the occasional, richly covered sofa. A large chandelier hung from the centre of the ceiling, and directly beneath, a marble fountain played water over the petals of floating, exotic red flowers. An occasional large frieze of Portuguese blue and white ceramic tiles and the mosaic black and white flooring completed an ambience of traditional Portuguese design.

Outside, the dusk blanket of the evening was covering the gardens, as the lights of the Village apartments on the next landscaped level took the place of the now elusive daylight. James approached the bar and was greeted with a smile. The large glass was already in the barman's hand. James also smiled and nodded, taking a reminding note from his name badge, that Emil was pouring the Coral beer. Smart couples were gradually appearing from all sides, indoors and out, set for an aperitif before they climbed the few stairs to the restaurant for dinner. A bearded pianist serenaded them from a grand piano on the mezzanine floor. It was five minutes past eight. James paid for his beer and thanked Emil. He would not be climbing the stairs to the restaurant. He took the corridor to the lift, made his way back down to Reception and waited in the lounge by the entrance. Just on eight-fifteen, he saw the taxi draw up beneath the giant palm. He opened the glass door, walked down the steps and took his place in the passenger seat next to the driver, who asked, "*Le Jardin?*" James smiled.

"Por favor," he replied.

On the downhill drive to the port, he noticed that one of the large cruise ships had departed, possibly on its way to the Canary Islands or North Africa. As they drove past the marina and on to Avenida Do Mar, James' eyes took in the panoramic hillsides, illuminated with endless strands of lights, from the many homes, occasional churches and hotels. Madeiran drivers were usually very polite to pedestrians and the taxi always drew up slowly towards the various automated zebra crossings on the way. Driving past the Promenade, the taxi turned left at the Museum of Electricity, then right onto Rua D. Carlos 1. They were now entering Funchal Old Town, as the car bumped over the narrow, cobbled street, restaurants to the left, the Cable Car station to the right, with the continuing Promenade and the Atlantic beyond. They drove on, reached the start of the Old Town and turned around, outside the gates to Hotel Porto Santa Maria.

James had once stayed there, in a first-floor sea view deluxe studio apartment, where one morning, he had gazed in wonder at, the *Queen Mary 2*, regally sailing by, just a few hundred yards ahead as he sat sipping on his pre-breakfast, strong black coffee.

In their black trousers, white shirts and black bowties, James saw the smiling waiters outside on the pavement. The taxi stopped. He paid and thanked the driver. The passenger door opened. He stood up, the door closed and the taxi headed back towards the town centre. He shook their hands, one by one, and was escorted to his table for one. "Boa noite, Mr James. Good evening. Welcome back."

The chair had been pulled out for him and was now politely pushed in, as he sat at his usual outside table beside the entrance. He turned to look up at the off-white wall to his left and admired the large, hand-painted frieze of a garden of brilliantly coloured flowers, above which was also painted, in the artistic script, the name of his favourite evening restaurant, *Le Jardin*.

Chapter 5
Cloaked in Red

'Same time, same place, same table.' Prior to his visits to Madeira, James would write a postcard to the manager and staff of the restaurant, informing them of his dates and would add the words 'same time, same place, same table'. The time was always eight-thirty. He was now seated at his usual table. A large glass of Coral beer was placed on the outside table at the entrance to, *Le Jardin,* Restaurante *Le Jardin*, in Zona Velha, Old Town Funchal.

Before eight-thirty, darkness descended on the island. Across the narrow cobbles of Rua D. Carlos 1, James could see the silhouettes of the local men playing cards at an old wooden table on the grass. The customary tramp was still there with his bag for life, seated against a large tree, feasting on the parcel of kindness from the restaurant, with the attentive, faithful company of his dog. Beyond, the distant horizon of the Atlantic was just visible, under a dark blue sky.

James sipped his beer. A spotless, large wine glass reflected the glow of a small, nightlight candle next to a short cactus plant on the table. Most of the other tables were occupied by couples of mixed ages, some of whom wore short sleeves in the warm evening air. James removed his blouson jacket and placed it over the back of the chair opposite. "Good evening, Mr James, you have your beer, I see." Like a younger, more handsome Poirot, Marcelo, the manager, stood at James' table and straightened his tie. The sparkle of his cufflinks was enhanced by the small candle flame. His well-groomed moustache and oiled black hair, combed straight from his brow, added to the friendly smile which exuded the typical warmth of Portuguese Madeiran hospitality. He walked over to a nearby table, lifted a wine bottle from its ice bucket and topped up the glasses of a receptive couple.

James took another sip of his cool beer. This was his evening place. He was part of it and it was part of him. Across the road, the tramp and his dog were slowly meandering towards the Promenade. He sensed a figure at his shoulder. As he turned, the always-radiant smile of the young waiter, Luis, looked down at him. "Good evening, Mr James, your menu." It was a polite formality to present a menu, for the waiters knew that on his first evening, James always ordered a starter of fresh Madeiran avocado with succulent prawns, followed by the main course of Beef Stroganoff, rice and tender, local asparagus. He salivated at the thought. "We have a new wine, Mr James. I shall show you." Luis went back inside and a few moments later, re-appeared and showed him a bottle of Portuguese red. "Versatil, Mr James, very nice."

"No more Nocturno?" asked James.

"No, Mr James, they finish your Dracoola wine. No more."

What a pity, thought James. For the past few years, James had enjoyed his bottles of Nocturno–*The Wine of The Night*, as they had translated it for him. James had thought that Nocturno was quite appropriate for his tastes.

Back in Edinburgh, some years before, James had been invited to a private, adults-only Halloween party, guests in costume, in a central wine bar. After some thought, he decided to make an impression and gradually put together his outfit. On the night of the party, he packed all the items in a plastic carrier bag, apart from the white shirt, black trousers and black shoes, which he wore. When he arrived, amongst other characters, he was greeted by Batman, Wonder Woman, Zorro and someone in a long white sheet with two eyeholes. "I'll just go and get into my costume," he said. "Won't be a moment." The Gents was conveniently empty. James placed his carrier bag by a washbasin. He took off his jacket and placed it under the bag. He looked in the mirror above the washbasin, then took out a small plastic bag from the carrier, opened it and removed some small items, black mascara, a narrow red lipstick, a set of plastic fangs and a gold medallion with a red ribbon. He skilfully applied the black mascara around his eyes and for blood dripping from his mouth, he realistically applied drops of red lipstick. He placed the red ribbon with the gold medallion around his neck and over the front of his white shirt, the top button of which was left open. He ran cold water onto his comb and styled his straight black hair backwards, swept over his skull. From the carrier, he took out a folded item of thin, black material. When he unfolded it with a sweeping gesture, it became a full-length black cloak, brushing the floor with its blood-red silk lining. He tied it around his neck, turned up the stiffened, large black collar and spread the cloak evenly over his shoulders.

James packed his jacket and the small plastic bag in the carrier. Lastly, he carefully inserted the plastic fangs into his mouth. *This is quite exciting,* he thought to himself. He turned around to look at the full-length mirror opposite the washbasin, raised his arms to reveal his glorious cloak in its horrific, black and blood-red splendour, secured his fangs and broke into a devilish smile. He picked up the carrier and took one more look in the mirror. In only ten minutes, he had totally transformed his appearance. Addressing his impressive reflection on his way out of the Gents, he wickedly uttered, "Come, James, it's party time."

On returning to the wine bar, it was Batman who spotted him first and boomed over the others, "My God, James, just look at you!" The others all turned from the bar and gazed in disbelief at the cloaked figure, who gratefully accepted a Bloody Mary from Wonder Woman. Dracula had arrived.

Chapter 6
A Likely Spy

James was finishing his beer when his artist friend Rui appeared and placed the avocado and prawns in front of him. As usual, the presentation on the plate was a sight to behold: a half avocado with shelled prawns and mayonnaise on top, avocado slices fanned out, with fresh tomato, lemon and olives and a whole prawn in the shell. *Succulent*, James thought. Rui poured a taste of wine into James' glass. "Just fill it up, Rui, please. I'm sure it's very nice."

"Yes, it is, Mr James. But no more Nocturno for Dracoola." James took a sip of Versatil and smiled.

"Very nice, thank you, Rui, full-blooded."

As James savoured his avocado, a couple stopped to study the menu displayed outside the terrace. They looked at it pensively, oblivious to Marcelo's quiet approach from behind, having had a short break for a cigarette near the recycling bins diagonally opposite. The couple sensed his presence and turned. "I can recommend..." His powers of persuasion escorted them to their table. As they took their seats, Marcelo introduced them to the man at the next table. "This is Mr James, our best customer." James finished de-shelling the whole prawn and politely greeted the couple.

"This is my wife Grace and I'm Tom."

"Pleased to meet you," said James. He was enjoying his meal and decided that conversation if any, could wait till later. The couple smiled and studied their menus. Another familiar face appeared with a moustache but also wearing a full black apron. In his hand, Antonio held a medium-sized shiny steel ashet, with small strips of fresh beef. "Very nice," said James, "but too much." The Stroganoff expert indicated two-thirds of the beef. James nodded. Antonio looked at him and smiled expectantly.

"With rice and tender asparagus. Half an hour?"

"Sim, por favor, please, Antonio." James took a sip of his Versatil. *Nice*, he thought pensively. "A bold, fruity palate, fresh black fruits, raspberry and plum. An aroma of black cherry and a hint of sweet spice. Almost purple in colour and with a lingering taste." James was by no means a connoisseur of wines, but he knew what he liked, and liked what he knew. In the next two weeks, he would get to know this wine very well. As he gazed at the candle's flame, his thoughts were interrupted.

"So you come here often, do you?" asked Tom at the next table. His wife, Grace, sipped her mineral water and listened.

"As often as possible," James replied with a polite smile. "They're threatening to open rooms upstairs, and I've been invited to be their first guest."

As Luis arrived with their vegetable soup, the waiter added, "And I shall ask the manager for the special moving chair on the stairs for Mr James." The couple looked at each other, unsure if they should say something.

"I'll see you later, Luis." But the waiter hastily went back inside, with a cheeky grin on his face. In addition to the restaurant's speciality flambe crepes, Beef Stroganoff was always cooked outside. Antonio had brought out the dish with the beef and all his other ingredients—olive oil, sour cream, seasoning, spices—and, of course, the essential brandy. James turned to watch the show. The expert poured some oil into the shallow pan, heated it to the required temperature, added the beef gradually and began to pour it over the heat, tossing the small strips till they were fully browned. Seasoning and spices were sprinkled on and mixed around the black iron frying pan slowly for a few minutes. The top was unscrewed from the bottle of brandy. Antonio poured a generous measure into the pan and tilted it with the mixture, letting the mixture connect with the heat of the hob. Antonio stood back, raised pan in hand as the flames leapt up to the stars and the darkness of the sky.

It was always a spectacle, not only watched and admired by James but also by the other diners. The flames died, Antonio returned the pan to a lower heat and slowly stirred in the sour cream. He stood in place for ten professional minutes, with no facial expression, but an occasional stir of the pan's contents, which were his one and only focus. Switching off the heat, he gave one final stir of the beef and cream mixture, removed the pan and went inside. Two minutes later, he came back out and served his customer. "Your Stroganoff, Mr James." The expert's customer looked down at his plate of tender strips of beef in sour cream and brandy sauce, a generous, regimental portion of tender, fresh asparagus and a white crescent moon of boiled rice. James looked up.

"Perfect, Antonio. Just perfect. Obrigado." As he put the first forkful of Stroganoff in his mouth and closed his eyes,

Antonio picked up the bottle of wine and topped up James' glass, before going inside, with a contented smile on his face.

Tender was the word. Tender strips of beef and oh-so-tender, fresh local asparagus all melt-in-the-mouth, with a perfect accompaniment of boiled rice. It was only when he had finished, had placed his knife and fork together on his plate and sighed with satisfaction that Tom, at the next table, politely looked across. "You obviously enjoyed that, James."

"You could say that again, Tom. Antonio makes the best Beef Stroganoff anywhere, I should think." He picked up his glass to sip some wine. "Cheers, bon appetit to you two." The couple both raised their wine glasses. Grace looked at James.

"We're here to celebrate Tom's retirement." As he took another sip of Versatil, Grace added quite unexpectedly, "He was a brain surgeon." James choked slightly on his wine, put down his glass, wiped his mouth with his napkin and poured a glass of his mineral water.

"Oh, how interesting, Tom. Pity you're retired. You might have had a look at mine," he chuckled, much to the couple's amusement.

"And you James, what do you do?" Tom asked.

"Now Tom, I'm not being impolite, but I have a long-standing policy that I never speak about work when I'm not working. Let's just say that I'm hired to use my brain, would you believe? Anyway, they seem to be happy with me and it pays for my food and drink. Cheers."

Rui made a timely appearance, stood between the tables and removed James' plate. "Dessert, Mr James? We have very nice, fresh Creme Caramel or maybe fresh Apple Pie? Also very nice."

"Rui, you always try to tempt me. And don't try to sell me any pictures tonight."

"No, Mr James, plenty of time for that." James smiled.

"Okay, let's go for the Creme Caramel. You know I only have an occasional dessert. Apple Pie, another time." Rui knew that James was a man of taste and discrimination when it came to desserts and as always, James slowly swooned at his excellent, fresh Creme Caramel, undisturbed.

His phone vibrated in his trouser pocket. Rui removed the dessert plate. "Large espresso and Macieira?"

"Por favor, Rui. Excuse me, I need to text a message."

He stood up, made for the pavement and crossed over the cobbled street for a better signal. He looked at his phone and texted a short message. Crossing back over, he greeted the waiters at, *O Tappassol*, next door, with a regal wave and a broad smile. In return, they politely bowed and also smiled broadly.

James sat down. "Nothing important," he said to the couple, who had an enquiring look on their faces. He put the phone back in his pocket.

He'd keep the remaining half bottle of wine for tomorrow. As usual, they'd write his name on the label and store the bottle safely. Tom and Grace had obviously enjoyed their grilled sardines and fresh vegetables, he had observed. They were now enjoying a complimentary small glass each of Madeira wine, as Grace decided she would have a word with Tom about James later. Grace considered herself a woman of considerable intuition and there was something about James that unsettled her slightly. And, after all, she had married a brain surgeon.

Grace raised her glass to James. "We mustn't be too late. It's been a long but lovely day."

"And we don't have far to go," said Tom, pointing. "We're just across the road, at the Hotel Porto Santa Maria. Lovely place."

"Yes," said James, "it is." Luis brought their bill, as they knocked back the last of their Madeira wine. Having paid, they rose to leave.

"We might see you again, James. But we like to try different places in the evening," said Grace, with a worldly expression on her face.

"Of course," said James. "It's been a pleasure meeting you both." He stood up and warmly shook their hands. Before they crossed over, he noticed that they looked both ways, just in time to see a vintage hire car with a driver pass by and slow down on its approach to the gates of Hotel Porto Santa Maria. But James didn't hear the short conversation, as the retired brain surgeon and his worldly wife eventually crossed over.

"He must be somebody important," Tom said, looking at his wife.

"Do you think so, dear? Personally, I think he's a spy."

Luis appeared at his table, with his espresso, a bottle and a brandy glass, into which he poured a generous measure. "Your Macieira, Mr James. Enjoy." Luis went to clear the next table. James drew the glass to his nose. He had long ago acquired a taste for the Portuguese brandy. He received the distinct aroma with its hint of honey, took a sip, rolled the amber liquid over his tongue and swallowed.

"Wonderful," he said quietly to himself. As he passed the table, Luis looked at James.

"No sign of rooms upstairs yet, Mr James, we need plenty of money. But I shall not forget the moving chair," he added as he disappeared inside. *Cheeky sod,* thought James, smiling, as he raised the espresso to his lips.

At eleven-thirty, it was still warm outside. People passed by along the pavement: couples, groups, possibly on their way to late bars for music, others to Hotel Porto Santa Maria and local families, some with sleepy infants across their shoulders, heading home to their small apartments. He looked across the road. There were four yellow taxis waiting for customers, three large ones with sliding doors and one smaller traditional Mercedes. The drivers of the first three vehicles stood together in a group, chatting and smoking cigarettes. The fourth driver stayed at his wheel. Rui had poured a complimentary Macieira into James' brandy glass. James produced his wallet to pay his bill. Luis stood outside on the pavement, greeting late-night passers-by. Rui nodded to Luis, who crossed the road and spoke to the fourth driver. Luis returned. "The small taxi is coming, Mr James." He watched the yellow Mercedes carefully reverse a few feet, turn into the road, drive onto the end, turn around, drive back and park outside, *Le Jardin*. It was a strategic operation and one, which James was accustomed to watching from his evening dining place. The boys at the restaurant knew James preferred a traditional taxi to the sliding doors of the larger taxis or as James referred to them as 'slicing doors', having almost lost a thumb in such a vehicle back home years before. As he entered the taxi, he turned to wave at the line-up of Luis, Rui and Antonio, standing smiling and waving from the outdoor terrace.

The driver turned to look at James, who said, "*Hole in One*, por favor." After the cobbles of Rua D. Carlos 1, they were now making their way along the smoother surfaces of the city centre, along Avenida Do Mar and the gradual uphill, westward climb. After his evening tastes of the Old Town, for James, the night was yet young.

Chapter 7
Let's Face the Music

They drove past the large fountain on the roundabout at the foot of Avenida Do Infante. At this late hour, it was turned off. During the day, however, the roundabout came to life around a central bronze globe with graceful, increasing arcs of water within a second framed circle of colourful plants and flowers. It was most certainly a local feature in this part of Funchal. As the taxi started up the gradual incline, they entered the silhouetted tunnel of tall trees, which stretched the entire length of the avenue. Tomorrow after breakfast, James would have his customary downhill stroll to the town centre, taking in Avenida Do Infante, Avenida Arriaga and their glorious daylight springtime display of purple blooms on the jacaranda trees. The avenue levelled off, as they drove on past Pestana Miramar and along Estrada Monumental. James had enjoyed the warm night air through the open windows on the drive uphill. Now in the distance, he could hear the sounds of live music drifting towards him. A few moments later, the car stopped. James paid his fare and thanked the driver. Straightening his black trousers, he opened the black iron gate, walked through and made his way into, *Hole in One*.

It was busy inside and on the outdoor terrace. James politely squeezed through to the bar. The staff recognised him, the Head Barman smiled, started to pour a large Coral beer and knew to open a tab. James thanked him and took his beer. He turned to look at the band and the male vocalist, who saw James and also smiled. *Hole in One*, was a very popular venue, with nightly live music until two in the morning. On Fridays, a good mixture of Portuguese and English jazz and popular music featured and attracted devotees of these genres, including James, who blended into the tempo, the rhythm and the infectious beat of the music. He could feel his feet already tapping on the bar floor, as he watched the dancers strutting their stuff on the available floor space. James looked around. He didn't see her. On previous occasions, he would watch and admire a tall, attractive red-haired lady dancing mostly on her own, but occasionally with a local man, who would join her from his stool at the bar. She was always well coordinated in her dress, shoes and jewellery. The last time he was here, James had taken his beer to a table closer to the dancing. He took a seat. The song was sung in Portuguese, the music was resonant and the solo lady in green occupied her usual place on the dance floor, oblivious to any other dancers and onlookers. She was focused on the beat and the rhythm of the dance. She may have been just a little older than James, but he was transfixed. Indeed, he had been bewitched. But there was no sign of her tonight. He turned to the bar for another beer and some polite conversation with the barman. James sipped his beer and watched the bar staff pouring drinks. Floor staff, men and women, glided gracefully throughout, sporting smart green polo shirts, with, the *Hole in One*, logo on the breast pockets. They served customers and collected empty glasses. There was a mixed crowd of dancers; locals, expats and tourists. A popular evening venue, especially at weekends, it could also be well patronised at lunchtime and in the afternoons, for a cool drink and an alfresco lunch on the usually sunny terrace. On occasions, staff would efficiently roll out a large, green canvas double canopy, to protect the garden furniture and customers, in the event of a short, subtropical shower.

The band stopped playing for a well-deserved short break and some refreshment. The dancers returned to their seats and also quenched their thirst. James looked along the bar and noticed the local man who occasionally danced with the lady, had arrived. He wore a navy-blue blazer, brown trousers and a smart, light blue shirt. He sat on a stool near the small stage, drinking a glass of white wine. The vocalist joined him and they clinked glasses. James placed a beermat over his glass and nodded to the barman. He passed the band and paid a visit downstairs to the Gents' toilet. As always, he stopped to admire the pictures of classic Cadillacs on the walls of the stairwell. The owner appeared from his basement office and passed James on his way upstairs, giving him a polite smile. Back at the bar, he removed his blouson jacket, rolled it up and placed it at his feet beside the bar. He tucked in his black, short-sleeved shirt and sipped his beer. He turned and looked at the black metal, distinctive silhouettes of golfers, which adorned the windows looking onto Estrada Monumental. He turned back to the bar to see which brands of whisky they had in stock. James was impressed by a full shelf of good malts. The band began to reform and took their places on the small stage. The vocalist introduced the next number. In no time, the strains of a familiar and ever-popular international song filled the air and soon filled the dance floor. James turned to see the action, and there she was, dancing to the rhythm and the beat of, *La Bamba*.

She was wearing a beneath-the-knee dress, with a tight bodice and flowing skirt as she turned in a circle. Laden with a gold chain necklace, earrings, bracelets and gold rings, she wore toeless canvas shoes to match her dress of jacaranda purple. As before, James was transfixed as she danced solo to the music of the band. He tried not to make it obvious and looked around at the other dancers. He wanted to join her, but the man in the navy blazer was watching her from his stool at the bar. Was he her husband? If so, James had better remain at the bar. The music stopped to a loud round of applause. As James sipped his beer, the vocalist ended his introduction to the next number. James recognised the opening bars of, Matt Bianco's-*Half a Minute. Come on, James, take a chance,* he thought to himself. He laid down his glass on the bar, placed a beermat on top, pushed in his blouson jacket on the bar floor and slowly made his way towards the small dance floor. Just then, the man in the navy blazer crossed over towards her and held her tightly, as they samba'd to the music. James stopped in his tracks and saw how they smoothly blended as a dancing couple, both entranced in the happiness of each other's musical flair. He tried to hide his previous intention diplomatically, looked at his watch and slowly made for the open door. It was quiet outside on the main road as he took in a few breaths of warm air. Turning, he went back inside, made for the bar and finished his beer. The Head Barman picked up a fresh glass. "Beer?" he asked.

"Por favor," said James, as he discreetly turned to see the couple swaying in time, her jacaranda skirt flowing in rhythm.

The party atmosphere continued. It was now one-thirty. James was getting tired after a long day. He took his last gulp of beer. The barman looked expectantly at him. "Macieira?" James nodded, smiled and took out his wallet to pay his tab. He would enjoy the short, ten-minute walk back to his apartment, for a good night's sleep.

The band eased into a slower tempo, as some dancing couples took the opportunity to enjoy a tender smooch. Others returned to their tables, well pleased with their Friday fling on the dance floor and now receptive to a welcome drink. The song was one of James' all-time favourites-*The Girl from Ipanema*. How he would love to dance with the lady. James lifted the brandy to his lips. When he looked in the large mirror behind the bar, he could see that the reflection of one specific couple had gone. He finished his Macieira, thanked the barman and left. As he turned into the Estrada, the final strains of the song drifted with him through the open doors and into the darkness of the night.

Chapter 8
Jacaranda, Mr James

James undressed, brushed his teeth, switched the air-conditioning to low and went to bed. The long curtains were partly open and through the lace screens, he could see occasional lights from other apartments. Perhaps, he thought, these were also people returning from their enjoyment of late-night music. James closed his eyes and drifted into a deep, contented sleep.

She was at the top of the Hollywood staircase, in a loose, full-length, flowing light purple gown, shoulder straps holding up a figure-hugging matching bodice. Her rich red hair draped her shoulders and she dripped elegant gold jewellery. She lifted her gown slightly, to reveal toeless, gold dancing shoes and let the gown slip back to the level of the top stair. Suddenly, from nowhere, a full-length mirror appeared in front of him. The man in the reflection was dressed in a full tuxedo and tails, white shirt, black bowtie and black patent leather shoes. A second look in the mirror took him totally aback, it was him, James Harris! "What am I doing here, dressed like this?" he asked himself.

He was startled by a woman's voice echoing from above, sultry and sexy, "James, darling, there may be trouble ahead…" Only now, on looking up, did he see the stunning vision, regal in a full-length gown of jacaranda blue. The music and Nat King Cole's smooth, velvety voice sounded above him. The woman slowly began her descent, looking at him and beckoning to him with a seductive 'come James' forefinger. The gown lavishly swept the staircase as she gradually got closer.

The music was reaching a crescendo. His throat had dried up. He couldn't speak. He couldn't move. "My God, what's happening?" he desperately said to himself. She reached the foot of the staircase and stood in front of him, her blue eyes and scarlet lips smiling wickedly as he continued to gasp. She raised the length of one side of her gown and gently placed it over his head and shoulders. "Come, James," she said invitingly, "let's face the music and dance." He couldn't breathe. He struggled to remove the gown from his head. He was choking, trying to free himself. Everything went dark and silent. An ongoing ringing sounded in the distance. One final, frantic struggle for survival made him break free and gasp for air. He threw the gown over his head, opened his eyes and looked around in confusion. It took a few moments for James to realise that he had been trapped tightly under the king-size duvet. He switched off his travel alarm, which showed eight-thirty. The dream had involuntarily exhausted him. He rose, put on his silk robe and opened the sliding balcony door. He stepped outside with a glass of water and inhaled several breaths of fresh morning air. "Oh dear, James, one drinky poo too many last night," he said quietly to himself. He sat with relief on one of the balcony chairs, reclined it slightly and looked up at the tall palm trees and the cloudless blue sky. Below, he heard the sound of gently lapping water as some guests enjoyed their leisurely, early morning swim. He admired the peach and purple petals of the bougainvillaea overflowing on both sides of his balcony. He turned to close the balcony door, preventing any of the occasional unwitting geckos from entering the apartment. He sipped his water and laid the glass on the circular, mosaic-topped table.

Apart from the latter stages, the dream had been quite enjoyable. He'd had visions of sweeping the lady off her feet, as in those classic Fred Astaire and Ginger Rogers black and white dancing films he'd enjoyed as a young boy. Instead, in his dream, the heroine had turned villainess and had almost suffocated him in a dance of death. He'd see that lady in a different light on his next Friday musical evening at, *Hole in One.*

After a light buffet breakfast and a strong black coffee on his balcony, James showered and dressed for his day in town. He made up his bed and tidied the apartment. He secured the balcony door and drew the screens. With blue sky and sunshine on offer, a white T-shirt, navy dress shorts and his sturdy sandals would suffice, but he nonetheless tucked a lightweight, aquamarine jersey around the strap of his shoulder bag, perchance it grew cooler later. He put on his faithful, blue-flecked fedora, at a slight tilt to the left. With all essential items secured in his shoulder bag and pockets, he put on his sunglasses and smiled at his reflection. "Have a wonderful day, Mr James," he said quietly and ventured out for his customary downhill stroll.

Staying on the left of the main road, he paused at the traffic lights, then crossed over and started his approach to Avenida Do Infante. Although there was no breeze, he held on to his fedora as he crossed the high bridge over the narrow

43

gorge. He had a clear view of, *Reid's Palace Hotel*, its subtropical gardens and the Atlantic Ocean. James had more than once enjoyed Reid's classic 'Afternoon Tea', with an accompanying flute of champagne, on the outdoor terrace, served by elegant young staff with crisp white tunics, well-polished brass buttons and black trousers.

He continued along and crossed over to the start of the avenue. As always, he admired the black and white mosaic pavements, inlaid with perfect, small volcanic stones. He stopped and looked up at the huge, *Savoy Palace Hotel*. James would pay a visit to admire the panoramic hillside views, both daytime and at night, from the roof terrace overlooking the ocean. He preferred smaller hotels but, the *Savoy Palace Hotel*, certainly ranked as a stunning establishment, despite its lack of aesthetic quality on the side facing the avenue.

Looking ahead, he could see the sweep of distant terracotta roofs of hillside houses. As always, James stopped before he began his walk down the sloping stretch of Avenida Do Infante and here it was, in front of him: the start of the spectacle of the long line of jacaranda trees, on both sides of the avenue.

As he continued his walk, he looked up at the vivid blue-purple, trumpet-shaped flowers, so familiar to this part of Funchal. The mosaic pavements were strewn with fallen jacaranda blooms, adding a distinct splash of colour to the black and white mosaics beneath.

James crossed over to the opposite side of the avenue and continued his stroll under the trees. The arcs of water spouted from the fountain, as traffic drove past the roundabout's integral floral display. He was now on Avenida Arriaga with, *Blandy's Wine Lodge*, opposite. He passed, *Cafe Ritz* and the

Golden Gate restaurant, both of which were his occasional haunts. But for James, as he continued towards the end of the avenue, dominated by Se Cathedral, his destination for a cool, thirst-quenching beer, was now a brief, right turn to, *Cafe Apolo*, with one 'l'.

As always, he acknowledged the right-hand wave of Pope John Paul, who faithfully stood outside the cathedral.

One of Madeira's best-known cafes, James would enjoy the first beer of the day at, *Cafe Apolo,* followed by a light lunch and coffee. Julio was surveying the outdoor tables when James appeared at the entrance.

The waiter smiled at James, approached him, shook his hand and cleared the small table just vacated by two local businessmen, after finishing their espresso coffees and small cigars. "Large beer?" James nodded and occupied his usual seat by the doorway, resting his shoulder bag on the other seat. This was the ideal place from which to watch the world go by and enjoy a quiet, civilised lunch. The cafe opposite and others on the sloping pedestrian walkway were also busy. The area led down towards Avenida Do Mar, the Promenade and the Atlantic beyond. To his delight, he could see the three musicians setting up their instruments in their usual stance, halfway down. Shortly, customers from all nearby cafes would be serenaded by the most wonderful, easy listening jazz guitar band. Julio appeared with his beer and placed it in front of James, whilst looking at his hat.

"What is it?" asked James. The waiter politely picked some small items from the brim of James' fedora and laid them on the table in front of him.

Julio smiled at the purple trumpet blooms, looked at him and said, with a proud air, "Jacaranda, Mr James."

Chapter 9
Lunching with Locals

James always enjoyed the ambience of, *Cafe Apolo*. It is a daily haunt of locals; mature, well-dressed ladies with elegant coiffures, sipping forever on small espresso coffees and large glasses of water and no doubt discussing the matters of the day; elegant, suited businessmen, cufflinks showing from the sleeves of their crisp shirts, enjoying a glass of wine, then espresso coffees and a glass of water, no doubt glad to get a break from the demands of the office. Some had a light, local savoury delicacy and a glass of wine for lunch. Most enjoyed a cigarette or a small cigar to follow.

There was continual conversation around the cafe. Tourists studied menus as waiters stood politely nearby, awaiting orders. An occasional family would seek a larger table for their lunch and a well-earned respite from their walking tour of Funchal. Excited children would ask for burgers and chips, which at, *Cafe Apolo*, James always noted to be of good quality, of course.

He looked up at the jacaranda trees. He took off his hat and placed it with his shoulder bag. He ordered a second beer. Looking towards the lower level of the outdoor terrace, he noticed the couple from, *Le Jardin*, Tom and Grace, wining and dining. He put his sunglasses back on and sipped his beer. Julio knew that after the second beer, James would have a light lunch and some red wine.

The pigeons wandered around the terrace floor, dodging between tables, hoping for some crumbs of comfort. A waiter would occasionally shake a cloth napkin at them, and they quickly escaped, fluttering up to either the jacaranda branches or to the higher levels of the cathedral opposite.

Having as always enjoyed the traditional tomato and onion soup, with a poached egg on top and garlic bread to accompany, he discreetly scattered some breadcrumbs across to and underneath the unoccupied table next to his. The birds were probably noting it already. He topped up his wine from the half carafe. As he sat back comfortably, the sound of the electric guitar echoed to the first bars of John Williams'- *Cavatina.*

How perfect, thought James. *How absolutely perfect.*

The cathedral bells struck one o'clock. Pigeons swept from the bell tower and dived, to land back on the jacaranda branches above the cafes. During the band's break, a loud horn sounded. James looked down to the Promenade and saw the large bow of, an *Aida cruise ship*, as it slowly began to leave the port. He saw Tom and Grace pay their bill and leave, heading for a closer look at the departing ship.

James sat back, adjusted his sunglasses and relaxed. He liked to be incognito on occasions. Julio signalled, "Coffee and?" A couple of minutes later, his large espresso arrived with a Constantino brandy, which is similar to Macieira and very acceptable as a substitute.

"Relax, James, relax," he said to himself, "and watch the world go by."

It was Saturday. He'd dress smartly for the evening. A sip of Constantino went down very well with the lazy, lunchtime jazz. When the band finished, James paid his bill and thanked Julio. He placed his bag over his shoulder and put on his fedora. He left, *Cafe Apolo*, and turned into Avenida Arriaga.

So began his leisurely stroll along the avenue past, *The Golden Gate*, past the well-occupied terrace tables of, *Cafe Ritz*, and on towards the roundabout, the arcs of water rising from the fountain and shining in the sun.

James gradually proceeded back up Avenida Do Infante, blissfully enjoying both the warm sunshine and the intermittent shade of the jacaranda trees.

After a shave and a shower, he wrapped the bath towel around his waist and looked at his just over six-foot broad frame in the full-length, sliding mirror of his wardrobe. His body was in fairly good shape for a fifty-two-year-old. Just a respectable hint of a good-living paunch, a fairly sharp jawline, a slightly aquiline nose, almost violet-blue eyes, quite a well-shaped mouth and, was that a vague beginning of a distinguished grey in his neat black temples? He seemed to be an almost of everything, but not quite.

Teeth brushed, face moisturised, body deodorant and aftershave both applied, his ablutions were complete.

Dressed in navy slacks, aquamarine Neru shirt and casual black slip-on shoes, he brushed down and put on his bottle-green woollen jacket, tucking a navy silk hankie in the breast pocket. A re-comb of his hair in the mirror and he was ready for Saturday evening. All necessary items secured on his person, he switched off any lights and closed the door of the apartment. Having decided to head up to the Roof Bar of, the *Savoy Palace Hotel*, no taxi was required just yet.

The view was indeed spectacular. Staff at Reception had politely greeted James after he had been welcomed by a smartly uniformed doorman at the entrance to, the *Savoy Palace Hotel*. Now, on the fourteenth floor, he was standing by the almost eye-level infinity pool, which seemed to blend with the night-time hillside lights of hundreds of Funchal homes, almost like an optical illusion. He turned and crossed over the terrace and looked out to the infinity of the Atlantic Ocean.

At the port, a large cruise ship was berthed, itself like a floating town, decked high with endless lights. Passengers keen to go ashore would be dining in Old Town restaurants or walking at leisure along the Promenade, perhaps looking for a restaurant in the nearby town centre or a cafe at the marina. Wherever they went, they were ashore and their ship was in sight.

James sat on a sofa with comfy cushions and sipped his beer. A waiter arrived with a small plate of savoury snacks, which he politely declined, keeping his appetite for his meal at, *Le Jardin*. Nonetheless, he gave the young man fifty cents, and he himself was, in turn, rewarded with a charming smile. Madeiran hospitality was consistently of a high standard, in James' experience and observation.

It was eight o'clock. He finished his beer and went inside to pay, passing along the outside walkway with its chest-high clear panels overlooking the gardens and pools, fourteen floors below. James stayed nearer the inner side of the walkway, dismissing a sudden feeling of vertigo.

Safely on terra firma outside the hotel, he hailed a taxi on the avenue. Ten minutes later, he was seated at his usual table at, *Le Jardin*.

Chapter 10
The Man at the Bar

James always enjoys his food and he particularly enjoys good soup. They do an excellent fish soup at, *Le Jardin*, but he'd keep that for another evening. Mind you, he was sure the chef put in extra fish in his soup, plus a bonus of some seafood. Did James complain? I should cocoa, dear. Tonight, he'd have the local fresh vegetable soup, his 'three a day' in one. For his main course, after studying the menu with a few sips of beer, it would be pork in wine with garlic and boiled potatoes. No dessert tonight, but of course, wine with the meal and coffee and Macieira to finish.

He had seen them when he had arrived, but as always, his attention was diverted as he took his seat and acknowledged the ever-polite waving of the waiters at the adjoining, *O Tappassol* restaurant. Both restaurants had the same owner, who occasionally appeared to see how the businesses were doing and to fraternise with diners, including James, to whose shoulder he would give a friendly squeeze. They were looking across at him, trying to attract his attention, in an endeavour to bring him over to their table for the usual. "Well, Hello ladies, here we are again. The Exclusive Club," and the customary, gentlemanly 'moi-moi' on their cheeks. But they are lovely ladies, James always thought. They too had their usual table and lived across the road at the Porto Santa Maria Hotel, "walking distance," Lesley would say, then add, "but stotting distance for her," referring to her companion Christine, who, to all accounts was fond of a gin or two and let out a flutter of laughter across to James. He always enjoyed meeting them, but now politely took his leave of them and returned to his own table for the arrival of his soup course, which as always, he proceeded to thoroughly enjoy.

He read his name, 'Mr James', on the label of the half-full bottle of Versatil wine from the previous evening. It washed down the melt-in-the-mouth pork perfectly. Another vintage saloon car drove past, tooted its horn and dropped its passengers at the hotel. From, *O Tappassol,* he saw 'Catman'—as James secretly called him—appear outside with a brown paper bag in his hand. He crossed over to the grass area, walked several yards to a clump of bushes and emptied out the contents of the bag carefully onto the grass. From the darkness but hidden from view, James knew that a cluster of feral cats each gave a gentle 'miaow' of thanks to Catman for their nightly alfresco dinner.

The Head Chef appeared for a welcome breath of air and smiled at James. He stood on the pavement, greeting occasional passers-by. Luis brought the coffee and brandy. Much as he enjoyed the Constantino at, *Cafe Apolo,* the Macieira for James had that essential taste of honey to enhance its smoothness.

The two ladies finished their complimentary glasses of Madeira wine and paid their bill. Placing their cashmere cardigans over their shoulders, they gave James a friendly smile and left. They crossed arm-in-arm over the cobbles, possibly heading for a nightcap in the Captain's Bar at Hotel Porto Santa Maria. "Mr James, we have very nice fish tomorrow," Luis enthused. "Shall I keep the whole sea bass for you?" The waiter did not miss the expectant look on James' face. "Of course, I shall take out the bones for you, Mr James, and serve the fillets with your vegetables."

"That would be lovely, Luis. Grilled as usual? I shall look forward to that." James gently held Luis' arm in a gesture of appreciation. The calmness of the late evening was about to be rudely interrupted. Waiters from both restaurants carried crates of empty bottles across the road, opened up the glass recycling bins and cascaded dozens of bottles to the insides. As always, it was an ear-shattering few moments. Those in the know, like James, placed a finger in each ear until the bin lids were closed. He would be gone before the bin lorry came later, to lift up the recycle bins and empty their contents in an even more ear-shattering performance. Well used to it, James had long since accepted this essential nightly part of Old Town alfresco wining and dining.

The small taxi was waiting. "Okay boys, see you tomorrow." The waiters waved to him as the car drove off along the road, towards the town centre and farther on to the uphill climb. "Now James, you must be a good boy tonight," he said to himself. Perhaps a late wine on the balcony was allowed, wearing his silk robe, listening to the silence of the gardens, the still pool below and looking towards the Atlantic, with the moon and the stars above. *Naughty boy, James,* he thought to himself. On second thoughts, he'd asked the driver to keep going and the taxi now stopped outside, *Hole in One.* After all, he justified his decision—it was Saturday night—and he wouldn't stay out too late.

The band was enjoying a break. Sitting on a stool at the end of the bar, the Saturday female singer took a welcome sip of white wine. James recognised her and as she looked across at him, he toasted her with his glass of beer. She was attractive, local, had a good voice and possessed a varied, popular repertoire of songs. Fridays and Saturdays were always busy and tonight was no exception; all tables were occupied indoors and on the terrace and only standing room at the bar, which suited James well. He was very much a 'standing at the bar person', except perhaps seated for a light lunch on the terrace or back at base on a sunny afternoon at a poolside table.

A man was seated at the bar, next to James, who observed that he was obviously well refreshed. His left elbow was dangerously close to James' beer, so he discreetly moved it along with his beermat. A few minutes later, the elbow had gradually slid farther along and again was almost touching James' glass. He decided to remove his beer and secure it in his hand, which was just as well. The elbow proceeded to sprawl along the bar, slip off, followed hastily by the connecting body, which crashed at James' feet in a state of unconsciousness. A stifled utter of alarm came from a lady at the nearest table, more in aid to rescue her large gin and tonic—as James observed—than as concern for the body on the floor. A barman and one of the floor staff hastily came to the rescue, checked that the customer was conscious and assisted him to a seat outside the entrance to get some air. After a short conversation, a taxi was called and the man waddled unaided to his transport home.

The lady vocalist had long, wavy dark hair and a lovely smile for her receptive audience. "If you want to dance," she said teasingly, "I think you will like this one." The band opened up the first few familiar bars of the song and immediately the dancing area was full to Pharrell Williams-*Happy*. Any outdoor space on the terrace came alive to the intensely infectious beat and rhythm of the celebrated song. A fever of happiness quickly spread throughout the animated dancers and also the spectators, who jived in their seats and clapped in time enthusiastically. At the bar, James realised his feet were also tapping in time and his hips were automatically showing just a hint of a sway. *Be subtle, James,* he thought to himself, wishing he was on the dance floor. As he spread his gaze around the dancers, there was no sign of her.

One more beer, then a Macieira for the road. By tradition, he'd be here for a light, early afternoon lunch on a Sunday. He occupied the vacant stool next to him and hoped that the previous occupant was now sleeping it off back home. A mellow Portuguese ballad serenaded the bar as patrons relaxed at their tables, enjoyed their drinks and friendly conversation. A few couples held each other close, savouring the social intimacy of their body language. His beer was almost finished and his brandy appeared. He paid his tab and decided to move outside for a short while, before heading back. The air outside was still warm. He chose a seat near the roadside entrance. A yellow taxi drove past, heading in the direction of the town. Even in the darkness, it was possible to see the silhouettes of the metal golfers beneath the moonlight.

Chapter 11
A Special Catch

A light buffet breakfast on the balcony is a good start to the day: fresh orange juice, a slice each of mozzarella cheese and mortadella ham, a hard-boiled egg, tasty local bread, butter, honey and a strong mug of Nescafe. *A fair sufficiency, James.* Below, the usual early towels on the usual sun loungers and the usual early swimmers doing their usual early lengths back and forth in the pool. *It is all very relaxing*, thought James, as he enjoyed his breakfast. People come here to relax and James was no exception, albeit incognito and far from his other life.

Sunday is a day of rest, he assured himself. Today would be an easy day: lift up to the pool terrace, a look at the panorama of Funchal, then a walk down to Estrada Monumental for a stroll along and a beer, before a light lunch at, *Hole in One*. A walk back to base and up to the Pool Bar for a couple of cool beers and some mid-afternoon sun. *Very civilised, James.*

He was feeling lazily refreshed after an hour in the sun. The few children who did come here were always well-behaved and older siblings or parents would reward the younger ones with a visit to the fridge cabinet situated by the Pool Bar and across from James' table. To see their young faces studying the large, tempting menu of ready-wrapped ice creams always made James smile. Had they sold a '99' vanilla ice cone with a chocolate flake, he might have been tempted. Having paid his tab, he headed back to his apartment, admiring the plants, colourful flowers and the small herb garden opposite the bar.

Just a quick shower to wash off the sun cream. He'd kept on his shorts by the pool, but on the reasonable privacy of his balcony, James would sunbathe in his black Speedos for a fuller tan. No shave today. *Go casual smart, James*, blouson jacket and Chinos, but with the purple and gold-patterned Turkish, short-sleeved silk shirt. A touch of casual class always made him feel comfortable. The bowtie would wait for another night. He buffed his black shoes, combed his hair, looked in the mirror and headed out for the evening.

People were congregating for their pre-dinner cocktails in the Winter Garden. James sipped his beer at the bar. It was 'Traditional Evening', a group of local singers and musicians in costume, men and women bringing an atmosphere of local culture to the visitors, albeit many of them regular visitors. James always smiled in acknowledgement as they passed him near the bar, but as he had his own plans for dinner, he'd decline the pleasure of their weekly performance in the restaurant. It was eight-fifteen–taxi time.

Marcelo, the manager, was standing at the entrance. He smiled, lit the candle on James' table, went inside and returned with James' beer. He adjusted the knot of his tie as he always seemed to do when he greeted James. "No starter tonight, Marcelo, but I think Luis has a sea bass for me."

"You are right, Mr James. It is swimming in the kitchen sink," he joked teasingly. "Nine-thirty?"

"Perfect," James replied, with a smile. "And a new bottle of Versatil, please." Two tables had been joined for a group of Germans. James overheard that they were from Hamburg and seemed to be from the business world, but he wasn't really listening in. They were happy, enjoying their food and wine. James enjoyed the sound of laughter. It was infectious and he broke into a smile as he turned and saw cheeky Luis.

Luis placed a gentle hand on James' shoulder. "I have the fish, Mr James, the sea bass."

"Yes, Luis, you will catch it at nine-thirty, take out the bones and serve the fillets with carrots and sauteed potatoes. The wine is ordered."

"Of course, Mr James. Only for you." The waiter smiled, showing a perfect set of white teeth. Needless to say, the fish was excellent. Luis' filleting skills were a treat for James to watch. He knew well that Luis took pride in them and always appreciated James' praise. Luis poured the wine. "Enjoy, Mr James."

"Obrigado, Luis, you are an expert." The young waiter raised his chin, adopted a professional expression on his face and returned inside.

A couple at the next table had been observing Luis' culinary preparations for James. After studying their menus, the man turned to James. "Excuse me, sir, what is your fish?" the American asked.

James swallowed a forkful of succulent sea bass and politely replied, "It's fresh local sea bass." The man looked back at the menu and then to his wife.

"I don't see that on the menu, my dear." James swallowed a forkful of carrots, looked to the next table and politely smiled.

"No, you won't find it on the menu. It's a special catch, of one." The couple looked at each other, as James took a sip of wine and resumed his meal. At that point, the young lady chef appeared on the terrace and smiled at James, who enthused about the fish. "Perfect," he said, returning a smile as she went back inside, satisfied. As he looked ahead towards the ocean, he saw the lights of the Porto Santo ferry reflected in the bay as it made its approach, heading for its berth at the end of the port. Later than usual, James observed, looking at his watch. He was enjoying this wine. It was a good replacement for his 'Wine of the Night'. 'Dracoola' approved and savoured the bouquet.

Along Rua D. Carlos 1, an accordionist was stopping at restaurants, pretending to play music. As the sound came nearer, James had already decided to give the man nothing if he came to his table. The same man would appear outside the cathedral, play a few pathetic notes of no description, cease playing, and then wander around the cafe tables with a tin cup for coins. And here he was now, doing the same. James waved him away as Luis appeared. "That man is hopeless," he said dismissively.

"I know," agreed James. "He's the same outside '*Cafe Apolo*' hopeless. Certainly not a good ambassador for the local musicians."

He gave Luis his remaining half bottle of wine to safe keep for the next evening. Two minutes later, the candle was reflecting on his glass of Macieira. He took a sip of his espresso. The restaurant was still busy. He gave the two ladies a polite wave as they were served their dessert. *Taxi straight back to base tonight, James,* he thought to himself. *Undress, silk robe on and a small glass of wine on the quiet balcony.*

Tomorrow would be a 'doing' day, a bit of walking exercise and exploration into the avenues and alleyways of the centre of Funchal.

Chapter 12
A Crystal Winestop

James' blue-flecked fedora blended well with the blue Portuguese ornamental tiled vignettes, showing scenes of old Madeira. The outside terrace of, *Cafe Ritz*, was busy with forenoon customers, some dwelling over a coffee, others intent on securing a table for lunch: smartly dressed locals, tourists, and James, with his blue fedora, royal blue Neru short-sleeved shirt—handmade for him in Jaipur, the previous year—khaki dress shorts and his faithful, sturdy walking sandals. He felt totally comfortable at his table for one, on Avenida Arriaga, with a strong black Americano coffee and a Macieira brandy.

Music at, *Cafe Ritz*, was always good, including the professional accordionist, who today was paired with an excellent saxophonist. James sipped his coffee and let the Latin American melody drift by in perfect harmony. The efficient staff took customers' orders, always attentive, polite and smiling. This was also a good place to watch the world go by, with a steady two-way flow of people strolling along the avenue.

Although he felt comfortably smart in his daywear, James couldn't help but notice the tall, fair-haired man at the next table, elegant in a navy-blue suit, crisp white shirt and red silk tie. He smoked a slim cigar, between taking sips of a large glass of white wine. He was reading a document, when a tall, attractive blonde woman joined him, kissed him on the cheek and sat next to him. He took off his tortoiseshell-framed glasses and laid them on an expensive-looking, brown leather briefcase on the table. The woman poured herself some mineral water and they clinked glasses.

Across the avenue, by the pond at the edge of the Municipal Gardens, some small children were cheerily tossing breadcrumbs to the receptive swans and ducks. On the pavement, drivers chatted by the stretch of yellow taxis, ever perceptive to a likely fare.

James paid and rose to leave. On the man's briefcase, he noticed a familiar, official-looking gold crest. As he continued along the avenue and approached the cathedral, James passed the headquarters of the Regional Government. He turned his head to the left and now recognised the crest on the highly polished brass plaque.

James stopped and looked at the cathedral clock. It was twelve-thirty. Se Cathedral, plain and simple outside, with white walls, terracotta roofing and a granite clock tower, nonetheless boasts a lavish and impressive interior as James knew. One of the island's oldest buildings, the cathedral can be seen from miles around and is therefore Funchal's principal landmark. It dominates the central shopping area, with black and white paving on the inviting, narrow streets, hosting occasional small cafes.

To his right, he could see that, *Cafe Apolo,* was quite busy. After an hour or so, he'd return for a beer, a light lunch and some wine. He crossed over to the small fountain, stopped and looked around the area, taking in the vivid blue jacaranda trees along the avenue. He turned left and proceeded up to the town's impressive main square with its dignified historic buildings, including the Jesuit College Church and Funchal Town Hall.

He was aiming for the old, traditional hardware shop, a virtual local, *Aladdin's Cave*, which sold both the obvious and the unlikely. Before that, he'd proceed along to the two busy thoroughfares, each of which has a central, narrow riverbed, carrying excess water from the mountains to the ocean. In spring, the riverbeds are covered by trellises of a vibrant bougainvillaea. Near the foot of the second thoroughfare, stands the Mercado Dos Lavradores, the famous *Workers' Market*. Today was Monday. For James, if it's Friday, it's market day.

On a Friday, the Mercado shows off its wares in all their glory. He always spends some time there on his second Friday forenoon and purchases some small items to take home. So, next Friday would be market day. Now it was time to retrace his steps. He took a narrow street off the square and recognised the old hardware shop a few yards downwards on the left. He stopped and looked at the windows on both sides of the shop, which were still painted in olive green. On a previous visit, he had bought some small traditional ceramic tiles.

Something caught his eye in the window on the left. Amongst some brass fixtures and ornaments, he noticed two plain, similar winestops made of glass. One was priced at twenty-one euros, the other at twenty-five euros. *Expensive pieces of glass*, he thought.

He wandered inside, remembering the narrow step on the left, and looking at the window display, he reached over and picked up both items. He saw on closer inspection what he had thought they were. He was aware of the young salesman standing beside him. "Are these Portuguese crystal?" James asked.

"Yes, sir." The young man politely smiled in answer.

"They are very nice," said James. "I shall think about it and come back."

He couldn't imagine that many tourists would come to a hardware shop for a souvenir and he hoped that the winestops would still be in the window on his next visit. He thanked the young man, left and continued down towards the cathedral and crossed over to, *Cafe Apolo*, for a lazy afternoon lunch.

Chapter 13
The Umbrella Man

The small table by the entrance was occupied. Indeed, there were no less than six established local ladies seated together, extra chairs having been borrowed from a larger nearby table. Small coffees and glasses of water were in place, and the ladies' conversation of the day was ongoing. James found a small table on the lower level and chose a seat where he could keep a diplomatic eye on the ladies. When there were signs of them eventually moving, he'd prepare to transfer to his preferred place. In the meantime, he'd have a beer, relax and watch the world go by.

The sunlight was fading. The waiters looked up and conversed. The ladies at the entrance table finished their coffees, rose from their seats and made to leave, each withdrawing a small umbrella from her handbag. James took his shoulder bag and beer over to the entrance and indicated to a waiter that he would occupy the table, which was partly covered with a sturdy, fixed canopy, the length of the restaurant frontage. The ladies scattered slowly in different directions, bidding each other farewell. The sky darkened as large menacing clouds gathered above. Most of *Cafe Apolo's* tables had large, thick white parasols, which were quickly raised by waiters. Customers drew in their chairs as near as possible to their tables. The first drops of rain fell, light and cool. Outside the cathedral—as James had anticipated—the umbrella man had already set up his stance at the foot of the steps and in front of the Pope. He called out his prices for umbrellas of different sizes, "small umbrella, two euros and big umbrella, three euros." The occasional subtropical rain of Madeira is a familiar feature of the island. He had no shortage of customers, who flocked to the cathedral steps to exchange two or three euros for shelter from the elements. James watched as the now heavy raindrops bounced off the restaurant's parasols and water ran down the sloping walkway between the cafes on both sides. Inside his shoulder bag, James had his small 'Diplomat' umbrella well-secured. However, he was well-protected beneath the canopy. He ordered another beer, with a cheese omelette and a half carafe of red wine to follow.

Within half an hour, the rain had stopped and the cathedral was bathed in glorious sunshine. The umbrella man methodically packed up his goods and left. James' lunch arrived. He unfolded his napkin and as he raised his glass of wine, looked ahead and wondered at the seemingly distant, colourful radiance of the huge rainbow over the Atlantic.

Chapter 14
Cracking Pistachios

The mosaic pavements were still wet when James returned along the avenue. In the sunshine, the rising arcs of water shone brilliantly from the fountain. Jacaranda blooms lay scattered along the uphill route, and plastic cape-clad tourists took photos from the passing open-top bus. It slowed down by the viewing point at Santa Catarina Park, taking in the gardens, the small lake, the bronze statues, the marina and the port, where two cruise ships had berthed earlier. The bus continued on its way, passing the elegant, pink Quinta Vigia, the official residence of Madeira's Civil Governor, in close proximity to the avenue, but behind locked gates.

Absolutely elegant, James thought to himself, as he looked at the handsome, circular glass dining table in the shop window. He always stopped here on his walk back to his apartment. The table settings of Portuguese china tableware, wine glasses and water glasses were a study in elegance, colour, coordination and style. Hand-embroidered placemats framed each individual set of bowls and plates. Even the napkin rings were colour coordinated, beautiful ceramic butterflies. How James could impress his friends back home with a dining arrangement like that. He took a photo as a record and headed back to base and his functional balcony furniture for a bit of afternoon sun.

James' balcony was ideally situated for mid-to-late afternoon sun. He reclined a chair slightly and laid a pool towel over it. With sun cream applied, a black baseball cap, sunglasses and black Speedos on, he was ready for some sun therapy. A cool can of beer from the fridge, a glass and a small bowl of pistachios were placed on the round, mosaic table. Perfect. He shook off his flip-flops, sat down, stretched out his legs and rested his feet on the narrow ledge. How peaceful. Only the murmur of polite conversations from the people on their sun loungers below, some reading kindles or paperbacks. He could hear quiet ripples of water, as a swimmer or two eased their way around the kidney-shaped pool. James' balcony was well framed in bougainvillaea, almost like the open curtains on a stage. He enjoyed a degree of privacy, so there was no real audience, just an occasional person below, scanning the subtropical surroundings from the poolside and perhaps catching sight of an anonymous man above, sipping his beer and cracking open pistachios.

James sat back and considered his morning: the elegant man at, *Cafe Ritz*, with the gold crest of the Regional Government on his briefcase; the Portuguese crystal winestops in the old hardware shop; the sudden downpour during his lunch at, *Cafe Apolo*; the umbrella man and the fallen jacaranda blooms on the slope of Avenida Do Infante. Later, after a beer in the Winter Garden, he'd taxi down to the Old Town and enjoy a pleasant evening at, *Le Jardin*. Tomorrow, after breakfast, he'd enjoy a leisurely stroll downhill into town, turn left and walk upwards, through the narrow streets and continue upwards to his old, classic haunt, *Hotel Monte Carlo*.

Chapter 15
Hotel Monte Carlo

It was a twenty-minute walk uphill to, *Hotel Monte Carlo*. James strolled along Avenida Arriaga, past the start of the taxi rank, the gardens, the pond with the swans and ducks, and the newspaper kiosk. He looked farther along to the cathedral. The clock showed almost noon. He turned left into Avenida Zarco. An imposing statue of Joao Zarco stands at the junction of the two avenues. Zarco, a fifteenth-century Portuguese adventurer, is widely credited with the discovery of Madeira.

He reached the top of Avenida Zarco, walked on past the familiar old church and continued directly through the narrow streets. He then stopped and looked up at the small name sign on the old wall, with an arrow pointing right.

More than twenty years before, after three weeks of clouds and non-stop rain, James decided he just had to escape. He hadn't planned a summer holiday at the time, due to financial commitments, but he just had to get away. An hour later, he had produced his credit card to Gary, his Travel Agent friend, who had looked on the Internet for a good deal. He had asked James, "Have you been to Madeira?"

"No," said James, "but I've heard it's very nice."

"Well, I can't tell you where you're staying, but if it's Madeira, it's bound to be quality," said Gary, with a knowing look. Assured of his return flights, airport transfers in Funchal and a good hotel, James thanked Gary and looked forward to a welcome change of scenery and some sun.

The flight had arrived in Funchal late afternoon. He saw his name on the card held up by the taxi driver. There were two ladies already seated in the back of the car. They exchanged a polite "Hello". James sat in front with the driver. "I think you are Hotel Monte Carlo, sir."

"Yes, okay," said James, slightly hesitantly. Half an hour later, they were heading downhill, into narrow streets. A left turn took them back up an even narrower street. They slowly drove through the tall, arched entrance with open steel gates and a tall palm tree on either side. The curved name above the arch showed, *Hotel Monte Carlo*. The taxi stopped at the foot of wide stone steps. Only the driver and James got out. The driver took his suitcase up the steps and laid it on the terrace. James thanked the man, gave him a tip and watched the yellow taxi make its way slowly back through the archway and out into the maze of narrow streets.

James stood and looked at the sweeping, slightly curved terrace, framed by stone balustrades, beyond which spread a breath-taking panorama of Funchal. He turned and looked up at the ornamental frontage of the hotel.

There were only two floors above the entrance and the ground floor; six triple-windowed rooms on the first and second floors, three on each side of a central, slightly prominent section, with a one-windowed centralised room above, and an arch below a small roof. On each side of this room, James saw the hotel's name in large block capital letters: to the left, "MONTE", and to the right, "CARLO". He noticed the light bulbs inset in the names, which as he would later discover, shine bright red in the dark, a night-time landmark.

The whole scene was like something out of an Agatha Christie novel. James could sense that the interior would be as decadent as the exterior.

He carried his suitcase up the few steps to the hotel's entrance. Inside, to the left, was an unoccupied Reception and a dining room. To the right, he saw a small lounge and a bar. In between an old lift and the stairs were a few glass cabinets displaying traditional artefacts. On the walls were old photographs of the hotel and a short description of its history.

As James would soon learn through his own personal research, *Hotel Monte Carlo*, has an interesting history.

The main building of, *Hotel Monte Carlo*, dates back to the start of the twentieth century. As a private mansion, it surveyed a magnificent view over the bay of Funchal and the Atlantic Ocean. James' basic knowledge of architecture identified such neoclassical elements as the neo-baroque and rococo decorative motifs in the front of the building. He also learned that in the Second World War, in 1940, a total of two thousand four hundred women, children and the elderly were evacuated from Gibraltar to Funchal. The building became a school, a British School for five hundred and eighty children from Gibraltar. They began to return to Gibraltar between 1944 and 1946. In 1964, the building opened up as, *Hotel Monte Carlo*, with extended accommodation, a small outdoor pool, and contemporary interior alterations and furnishings to create, *Hotel Monte Carlo*, as an iconic, quality hotel.

The European upper classes visited Madeira over the years. Some stayed at, *Hotel Monte Carlo*; aristocrats, artists, businessmen, poets and international politicians. The hotel was taken over in 1985. Today, *Hotel Monte Carlo*, continues to be considered as a small hotel of charming character.

A man quietly appeared from the bar area, dressed in black trousers, a white shirt and a black bow tie. His name badge indicated 'Paulo, Reception and Bar'. "Welcome, you are Mr James?" After the formalities, James was issued with a key. "You have Room 19. Take the lift." James did as he was instructed. Room 19 was classified as the third floor. He turned the key and opened the door. It was quite a large room with a double bed and ensuite bathroom. He put down his suitcase and closed the door.

When he went over to the window with two vertical openings, he gasped. "My God, James, Room 19 is the room at the top." The panorama of Funchal and the Atlantic Ocean beyond was absolutely breath-taking.

James decided then that he was in love with, *Hotel Monte Carlo*.

And here he was now, more than twenty years later, sitting at a table on the hotel's terrace, with a large Coral beer and the panoramic view around and beyond. James had returned to stay here on three more occasions, before investing in his timeshare apartment at Miramar. He knew this terrace well from alfresco breakfasts, late afternoon beers in the sun, and after evening meals at, *Le Jardin*, his nightcap Macieiras under the red, illuminated name, the moon and the stars.

James remembered one late evening or had it been early morning? Savouring the warm air, gazing at the night-lights of Funchal, and indulging in a second nightcap. It had been so relaxing. He had felt a gentle hand on his shoulder. "Mr James, you are sleeping," Paulo had said, with a polite smile. "I think all of Funchal can hear you," he added, with an additional, polite sweep of his hand. "I think Room 19 is waiting for you."

Oh dear, James had thought to himself. *I must have been snoring.*

It was one-thirty. James waved thanks to the waiter and left enough money for his beer and a tip. He looked at the view, turned and looked up at the hotel. Somehow, he knew he would be back again to stay at, *Hotel Monte Carlo*. He picked up his shoulder bag and gave his fedora a discreet tilt to the left. He walked down the steps, under the palm-fringed arch and headed downhill, through the narrow streets, to the town centre.

After a pleasant walk to whet his appetite, a light lunch at, *Cafe Apolo,* was now most certainly on the menu.

Chapter 16
Quietly Captivated

The attractive young lady exuded experienced authority. She clasped a slim blue folder at her side and strode confidently past, *Cafe Apolo*. She stopped and as she did so, the crocodile of schoolchildren following her came to a polite, almost military halt. James didn't count them, but there must have been about twenty young girls and boys, keenly holding clipboards, paper and pencils at their sides. They were about twelve years old, dressed in school uniform, but free of blazers in the warmth of the afternoon sun.

She turned, looked at them, and smiled. Her smile was reflected by her pupils, who obviously loved their teacher. She asked one or two questions, young hands stretched into the air and young eyes opened wide. Satisfied with their answers, she clapped her hands, nodded to her proteges, turned, held up an arm and indicated for them to follow.

James was quietly captivated by the scene as he approached the cafe.

His preferred table was occupied by four of the local ladies. However, the ever-attentive Julio separated two adjoining tables, so that James had a table for one, after all. "Hello, Mr James. Como esta? How are you today?"

"Fine thank you, Julio. Oh Bem, obrigado." He took his seat and looked forward to a cool beer.

The flamboyance of these slightly mature ladies always drew James' attention. He would discreetly observe them, their elegant, carefully coordinated clothes, immaculate hairdos, almost theatrical jewellery, facial expressions and hand gestures, all in a tasteful form of Portuguese potpourri.

He decided on no lunch today. However, he fancied a couple of small custard tarts with his coffee and brandy, after finishing a second beer. These small, home-baked, bowl-shaped tarts are a traditional sweet speciality: light, flaky pastry, a slightly browned sweet custard filling, melt-in-the-mouth, perfect with an espresso and a brandy. Plenty of pastry crumb leftovers for the ever-expectant pigeons.

A walk along the Promenade, towards the marina, took him past cafes, restaurants, and the African ladies selling sparkling, brightly coloured jewellery, in the open air. James stopped to look at the yachts of different sizes, the occasional fishing boat, the tourist catamarans for dolphin and whale spotting. James had done that, on one of his more adventurous escapades.

He looked across and admired the P&O cruise ship, *Britannia*, as launched by HM The Queen. The sleek ship, with its Union Jack livery on its bow, was berthed along from the old fortress, now a restaurant by day and disco by night, as James had discovered on a previous visit.

He tilted his fedora to the sun and prepared to head up the hill, back to base for a snack, some white wine and some sun on his bougainvillaea balcony. *How decadent, James,* he thought.

Chapter 17
The Police Van

There was just a hint of a chill in the evening air. James kept on his green, woollen jacket as he sipped his beer and studied his menu. He would occasionally forego the main course and have two starters instead, notably if one of them was the fish soup, an excellent warmer and very filling, in his own experience. He'd follow it with the juiciest sweet melon and very tasty Parma ham. Perfect. And wine, of course. He looked across at Lesley and Christine, sipping their cocktails, and decided to go over and have a quick chat, thereby killing four birds with one stone. He had observed that Tom and Grace were seated at the next table and speaking with the ladies. "Hello, James," said Lesley, beaming a smile and turning to their neighbours. "This is Grace and Tom," she said, looking at the couple. "This is James, a good friend of ours from 'Le Jardin'."

"Oh yes, we've met James," said Grace, studying his green, woollen jacket for any hidden wires.

"Oh, that's nice," said Lesley. "You know, James, when you look at Tom, you'd never think he was a brain surgeon, would you? I said he should have a quick look at hers," and looked over at Christine, who cackled heartily. James felt his phone vibrate in his trouser pocket.

"Oh, you'll need to excuse me, duty calls. Nice to meet you all again. Have a lovely evening." He crossed over the road for a better signal and returned a wave to, the *O Tappassol,* waiters next door.

"You know ladies," said Tom quietly, "Grace thinks James is a spy."

The two ladies looked at each other. "Oh my," said an astonished Christine, "I do hope I didn't give away any state secrets through the gin," and heartily cackled again. Lesley gave her a look of mock scorn. As James returned to his table, they watched him remove a wired device from his ear and phone and tuck it into the breast pocket of his jacket.

Grace looked at her husband with a confident air, and whispered across the table, "What did I say to you, Tom?"

As usual, the fish soup was more like a fish stew, with generous, small fish pieces, some seafood and vegetables. Very hearty indeed, and very filling. James asked Luis to leave the melon and Parma ham for another half hour. As he sipped his wine, he looked towards the Promenade. The silhouettes of the bearded tramp and his dog were approaching the grass area with the tall tree. Across from the tree, at the rustic table on the grass, he saw the shadows of the silent card players. The tramp and his dog sat a few yards away under the tree, awaiting their nightly food parcel. A sinister-looking police van had appeared and had parked a few yards along from the usual taxis.

As Luis served the second course, James asked him quietly about the vehicle. "It is your taxi for later, Mr James." He smiled, topping up the glass of wine and returning inside.

Cheeky sod, thought James, breaking into a smile. He didn't hear Grace whispering to Tom, pointing to the mysterious van and then nodding towards James, with a confident expression on her face.

As James sipped his espresso, followed by a sip of Macieira, he wondered perhaps if the Police had received a tip-off of some illicit, public gambling nearby and were quietly observing. As Luis poured his usual complimentary brandy, the van quietly reversed, turned and drove back along Rua D. Carlos 1, and towards the town centre. Luis feigned a serious look at James. "They will come back another night, Mr James," he said, glancing across the road. "Be sure."

Back on his balcony, with an indulgent, small glass of white wine, James tightened his silk robe against the night chill. The occasional lights of an apartment showed through the tall palms. He looked at the stars above and ahead as part of Friday's plan: a walk downhill into town and onto Mercado Dos Lavradores, the famous 'Workers' Market'.

Chapter 18
Market Day

Having walked into town, he now crossed the two central thoroughfares and the narrow bridges over the bougainvillaea and trellis-covered riverbeds, before coming to the peach-coloured distinctive building of Mercado Dos Lavradores–the Workers' Market.

For James, Friday is always market day. Although open Monday to Saturday, Friday is the busiest market day, when the whole market is occupied. Workers from all over Madeira head for Funchal, farmers, traders and fishermen, who expertly set up their produce and wares for local customers and tourists. The building has two floors and has an open roof, with a cafe-bar terrace. The large basement houses the fantastic fish market. James had always made a point of going downstairs first, to walk around and marvel at the different harvests of the ocean, including huge slabs of tuna, swordfish and the menacing, black-skinned eel-like espadas, a metre in length and with long, needle-sharp teeth. Despite its appearance, espada is a favourite local delicacy in restaurants, its white meat either poached, or its fillets fried and served with banana–a popular choice.

James went back upstairs and stopped to look down again at the marvellous harvests of the Atlantic. He turned into the central part of the market and wondered at the myriad of stalls on both floors, with a central atrium and the gallery above: exotic, local fruits and vegetables, of all shapes, colours and sizes. James stopped and looked up at the curtains of red chillies, hanging above the harvests of the land and expertly displayed in local, handmade wicker baskets, the stalls filling the entire area. Butchers' stalls, wicker shops, leather goods, handicraft shops, cake, wine and confectionery shops can also be found around the perimeter of the market.

As usual, he took in the whole scene on both floors before passing through flower sellers' stalls, situated inside the market's entrance. For a few friends, James always purchased small, sealed honey cakes, bolo de mel; bags of sweets made from local fruits, some tomato seeds and flower bulbs. All easy to pack in his suitcase and not too heavy. His customary bottle of Macieira would be a duty-free purchase at the airport.

On his way out, he looked up to admire the traditional blue and white tile vignettes, depicting scenes of workers from days gone by in Madeira. "Right, James," he said to himself, "that's one mission in town accomplished." He had two more missions before lunch. Next stop, winestop. He crossed back over and headed for the square. James turned left into the narrow street, walked down a few yards and stopped outside the old hardware shop.

He looked in the left window. Only one winestop was on display, the hexagonal one with a circular centre; plain, clear crystal and priced at twenty-five euros, the dearer of the two original winestops. He entered the shop, made for the window display and picked up the winestop to study it more closely. As on his previous visit, the young man came over. "Did you sell the other one?" James asked.

"Yes sir, a nice lady bought it yesterday."

"In that case, a nice man will buy this one today," James said, with a smile.

"I'm very fond of red wine and have several winestops, but this is a very special one, Portuguese crystal, plain, simple and beautiful and from a very good, traditional shop." The young man smiled in thanks.

James added, "You speak very good English."

The young man smiled again. "The shop belongs to my family, for many years. I work here to help sometimes, but I teach at the university in Lisbon."

"My subject is Physics." James nodded in acknowledgement and handed over the winestop. They both went over to the shop counter. The young man carefully wrapped the piece of Portuguese crystal firstly in some tissue, then in a small piece of a local newspaper, sealing it with Sellotape. James handed over his twenty-five euros and secured the winestop in the small, inside zip pocket of his shoulder bag. "Of course," said James, "I shall not use it for wine. I shall place it on my west-facing windowsill and in the late afternoon sun. It will shine the colours of the rainbow in my room. I know."

The young physicist smiled and knowingly said in acknowledgement: "Like the rainbows of Funchal. I also know." They smiled at each other and shook hands. James left, put on his sunglasses and walked out into the warmth of the early afternoon sun.

Chapter 19
The Main Attraction

He had often stopped to admire the elegant gents' clothes in the windows of, *Phoebus*, across from the cathedral, but he had never indulged in the purchase of a distinctive shirt in patterned shades of blue that he had sorely been tempted to buy on a previous visit. Tonight was his second and only other Friday in Funchal, on this occasion. Glad rags' night needed a bowtie and he'd decided not to bring one, but to treat himself to one here. The lady behind the counter greeted him and on listening to his request, politely passed him to a smart, senior salesman, perhaps the manager. When James stated what he was looking for a flat square box was produced from beneath another counter. The salesman removed the lid to reveal a small selection of bowties, mainly in plain colours, but also a few with simple designs. But he saw it, the only one with an almost classic, silver leaf motif panel, attached to a navy, framed background. *Elegant*, James thought, and perfect for his lilac-blue dress shirt and silver cufflinks. It was settled. The second mission was accomplished and the very satisfied customer walked outside, turned right, crossed over to the cathedral and headed for his third mission, lunch at the free table by the entrance to *Cafe Apolo*.

James blamed his lazy afternoon on the jazz guitar music, absolutely nothing to do with a couple of large Corals, followed by a fabulous cheeseboard selection for one, with sea salt crackers, grapes, Parma ham and a half carafe of red wine to wash it down with. Would he indulge in an espresso and Constantino brandy to finish off? Strains of Santana came drifting along from the band. "Come on, James," he said to himself. "Live for the moment." Julio passed by, carrying a tray of empty glasses. He smiled. "Coffee, Mr James?" It was understood. By the cathedral steps, an old man pushed a baby buggy, holding two small, satisfied, reclining dogs as if passengers travelling in style, in the direction of Avenida Arriaga and the jacaranda trees. James would be heading that way shortly; a leisurely stroll up the hill, back to base and preparations for his Friday night out.

But of course, James also enjoys his 'take it easy day': wake up coffee on his balcony, light breakfast on the balcony, freshen up, into shorts and a T-shirt, head along to, *Hole in One,* for a civilised liquid lunch on the terrace, near the feature, full-sized Cadillac, a stroll back to base, a beer by the Pool Bar, in the shade of the tall palm tree, then back to the apartment, slip off the shorts, T-shirt and sandals, then on to his balcony for a glass of white wine, a small bowl of pistachios and some semi-private sun, wearing his black Speedos. Simple as that, and oh so easy. "Pure, take it easy decadence, James," he would say to himself, with a tilt to the left of his matching black baseball cap.

"Look out the glad rags, James," he said aloud: black cotton jacket, grey trousers with a navy fleck, lilac-blue dress shirt, silver cufflinks, the navy and silver bowtie, black shoes and the lilac-blue silk breast pocket-handkerchief. Showered, shaved, ablutions complete, with just an extra spray of aftershave, he looked at himself in the full-length mirror. "My God, James, Bond has nothing in it." He swept his comb through his hair, including the distinguished grey flecks, locked up, left and headed for a pre-taxi beer in the Winter Garden. The barman politely admired him as he handed him his beer.

Having admired the regal lines of Queen Mary 2 at the port, James' taxi now approached, *Le Jardin*.

Marcelo, the manager, took a mental picture of James in his glad rags. He looked him up and down and smiled with a polite twist of his neat, black moustache. "Mr James, you are elegant and the smartest man in Funchal tonight, I think."

"Well thank you, Marcelo, but of course, you are always smart." The manager acknowledged the compliment with a polite nod and went inside to fetch a large Coral for his best customer. As he sipped his beer, James noticed that Lesley was sitting on her own. As Luis passed by, he quietly asked him where Christine was.

"She is not here tonight, Mr James," and added quietly, "Too much gin at the hotel, I think." James smiled and ordered the duck. No starter tonight, but he'd treat himself to the excellent fresh apple pie and cream for dessert. Lesley looked over and he gave her a cheery wave.

The slices of duck breast, served with a small jug of Madeira wine and fresh orange juice sauce, were succulent, accompanied by sauteed potatoes and broccoli, washed down with a couple of large glasses of Versatil. He'd also savoured the slice of cinnamon-flavoured apple pie with fresh pouring cream, before his customary espresso and Macieira. He looked over to his black jacket, hanging on the seat opposite, showing the lilac-blue silk handkerchief in the breast pocket. *Marcelo was right, James, you are quite possibly the most elegant man in Funchal tonight,* James thought, permitting a discreet smile to himself. He gently touched the symmetry of his Portuguese bowtie and noticed that Lesley was donning her cashmere cardigan. He rose and politely went over. "No Christine tonight?" he inquired.

"Eh, no," she replied. "She's feeling a bit off tonight."

"Oh, that's a pity," James sympathised. "Do give her my best wishes and we hope she'll be on for tomorrow." After receiving the obligatory 'moi-moi' from James, Lesley left for the hotel across the road. James returned to his table, squared up his bill and sank the last of his pleasantly warm brandy. The taxi was waiting. He saluted his friends as he turned to the driver. "*Hole in One,* por favor." From, *O Tappassol*, next door Catman emerged, slowly crossed over the road, with his food parcel for the feral pussies, hidden in the bushes. As his taxi headed uphill, James was quite unaware that for him, Friday night would be much more than music night.

He managed to find a space at the bar, albeit not as near to the band yet as he'd have preferred. The atmosphere and the ambience brought James back to life, after his relaxing meal at, *Le Jardin*. It was eleven forty-five. More than two hours of his Friday night to enjoy. Tomorrow would be a 'take it easy day', until the evening, his second and last Saturday. He took a sip of his beer and looked around, as the male vocalist kept the tempo going with a Portuguese foot-tapper. James felt his toes tap through the leather of his shiny black shoes. How he would love to dance. He looked along the bar. The man in the navy blazer was sipping white wine, as he sat near the band. Discreetly, James scanned the dancing area for her. No sign. The band stopped for a short break. The barman looked at him in anticipation. James nodded and his second beer was poured. "Take it easy, James," he said to himself, "the night is yet young." He paid a visit downstairs. He admired his reflection in the Gents' mirror. Elegant, Marcelo had said. The bowtie was the finishing touch. With a couple of sweeps of his comb, his hair was to his satisfaction. An older man emerged from one of the WCs and looked at James as he washed his hands. "You moost be the main attraction tonight then," he said smiling.

"Oh, I don't think so," said James bashfully. "I tend to indulge myself on holiday weekends."

"Well then," said the man enthusiastically, "Ye can indoolge yerself in one o' them loovly ladies oop there. That should be no problem for a man like you." James smiled and went back upstairs.

The band was warming up. The singer adjusted the microphone. A moment later, they broke into the unmistakable introduction to, *La Bamba*, an obvious Friday favourite. James noticed the man in the navy blazer lay down his wine and stand up. The floor began to fill as he made his way across. James turned. In her usual space, immaculately dressed in an avocado green, flowing knee-length dress, matching casual shoes and strings of rainbow-coloured necklace and bracelet beads, Ginger Rogers was joined by her dancing partner. James turned back to the bar. He studied her reflection in the large mirror. This was the hypnotic woman who had bewitched and captivated him, to the point of near suffocation. *Snap out of it, James,* he thought to himself. *It was just a dream.* He sipped his beer and turned back to watch the dancers and spectators applaud when the music finished.

At that moment, the female vocalist arrived with a man friend. They sat on stools kept for them beside the band, who were now playing, *Happy*, to a very receptive and animated crowd of dancers. James' feet were tapping and his hips were tastefully and discreetly swaying as he watched from his place at the bar. He wished Navy Blazer would evaporate. When the music stopped, the band took another short break. The lady vocalist, usually appearing on Saturday nights, spoke to her Friday counterpart. They opened the songbook by the microphone stand, turned over a few pages and nodded to each other.

It was twelve forty-five. He'd stay for one more hour, then head back for a good night's sleep. He saw Navy Blazer go downstairs. Both vocalists stood up after a short conversation with the musicians, Spanish guitar, saxophone, keyboard and drums and waited for the first few bars of the guitar to warm up. He heard the slow introduction to, *Senorita*. An international hit for Shawn Mendes and Camila Cabello, this was a song James could most certainly dance to. The mellow strings of the guitar quietly resonated around the bar and the floor began to fill. He could just go over, blend in with the crowd and discreetly strut his stuff. His confidence was sufficiently boosted by beers, wine and brandy already consumed earlier. *Go on, James, be a devil,* he thought to himself. He placed his beer on the bar, put the beermat on top, looked at the winking barman, turned and made for the dance floor. He politely squeezed through a few dancers and unwittingly found a space opposite another solo dancer. She beckoned him with a slim, tantalising forefinger and its pointed avocado-painted nail. James was trapped, helplessly caught and consumed by the silk of Ginger's salsa avocado web.

Chapter 20
Fred and Ginger

His knowledge of salsa went back to a few years before, when he had been coached the movements by a lady friend in the basement of, *Salsa Cellar*, in Edinburgh. Now, here he was in a popular bar in Funchal, dancing literally with the lady of his dreams. As a couple, they blended well, their movements led by the lady and followed by the man. They needed space and the nearby dancers politely stopped to watch, admiring and enjoying the skill of this handsome couple, moving to the rhythm of the music and the song.

The band watched as they played and the vocalists sang with added gusto. As the music continued, Fred responded to Ginger's sway and she to his coordinated response. Unexpectedly, her mouth brushed his ear as she whispered, "Do you like your senorita?" James smiled as their eyes met. They danced on until they lavishly flourished their final move of the dance and stopped to pose for the crowd. James held her around the waist and politely kissed her on both cheeks. The applause was deafening. The band and vocalists clapped enthusiastically. James was in Heaven and this was his living dream.

Suddenly, he felt a tap on his shoulder. It was Navy Blazer. "May I have my wife back, please?" he said with a smile. "We have to go, the plane for Lisbon is tomorrow. The car is waiting." James turned to his dancing partner.

"Thank you, that was wonderful. I shall never forget it. May I ask your name?"

"My name is Carmo. My husband is Filipe. And you?"

"My name is James. It was a pleasure to meet you both, and of course, to dance with such a beautiful lady, Carmo. You taught me a lot. Thank you."

"It was also a pleasure for me, James. You are an unusual man." James shook hands with Carmo and Filipe, who then both made for the open exit, where outside on the Estrada, a dark limousine was waiting with a uniformed chauffeur holding the rear door open.

James turned to the bar. He wondered who the couple was. They certainly seemed almost aristocratic. Perhaps local royalty letting their hair down? European royals were well known for socialising with the people. Yes, James would remember this evening's dance with a difference.

The Head Barman guessed his thoughts. "Very big businessman in Madeira, a very nice couple. Popular with the people. One more beer, my friend, and then the Macieira?"

"Por favor," James replied. "I need to get my breath back."

"You were very good," said the barman. "Touch of class, if I can say."

"Well, thank you," said James with a beaming smile. "I really appreciate that." *Perhaps there's just a hint of the aristocrat in you, James,* he thought to himself, giving a discreet, slightly regal wave and a smile to the customers.

As the limousine made its way uphill to the mansion behind large, metal gates, Filipe took his wife's hand warmly. "Thank you, my darling Carmo, for dancing so wonderfully with the gentleman. The people like you. I always tell you I am a lucky man. You are good for my business."

Carmo squeezed his hand in turn. *The gentleman was good for me,* she cheekily thought to herself, as she leaned over and kissed her husband on the cheek. James was indeed an unusual man, and she would like to have taught him more…

He was still quietly revelling in his moment of glory when he saw the reflection in the large mirror behind the bar: the man from the Gents' toilet earlier, who now faced him at the bar. "Eee, by goom, that was really soomthin! Ye were joost like Fred Astaire and Ginger Rogers!" James smiled, thanked the man and paid his tab. After a sip of his beer, he lifted the Macieira to his nose and let the aroma of the mellow, amber liquid slowly waft through his nostrils. He occupied a stool and watched as the band slowed its tempo and couples closely swayed to a sultry rhythm.

"Well, Fred," he said to himself, with a satisfied smile, "You finally did face the music and dance!"

Chapter 21
Canopies and Cadillacs

An easy day. After a light breakfast on his balcony, James decided to take a stroll around the subtropical gardens of Miramar and the Village gardens on the upper level. The grounds were immaculately maintained, but with a subtle, clever appearance of natural beauty in the wild. Years before, he had joined a group of people on a small, chartered yacht to visit a private side of the island, with plantations of bananas, avocados, mangos and papayas. A small wine refinery processed the produce of vineyards into fine wines for tasting. They'd had a wonderful alfresco lunch on the beach, with freshly caught fish, local wine, the freshest of local vegetables and fruit salads, before a lazy return sail on the Atlantic and around the coast.

And here he was now, in the gardens, looking at two banana trees, positioned amongst exotic flowers, with a multitude of colours, shapes, sizes and scents. On his walk along to, *Hole in One,* later, he'd pass a small plantation of bananas opposite, *Villa Cipriani*, the popular Italian restaurant belonging to, *Reid's Palace Hotel*. He'd often wondered if these bananas were harvested and sold at the Mercado. He crossed the bridge over the pool and entered the main section of the small Village, with its traditionally designed studio apartments. Again, the landscaping was well planned, yet totally natural. An occasional motorised trolley would slowly be driven along the narrow, pink brick pathways, loaded with dead leaves and flowers from the various trees, bushes and plants. He walked full circle and arrived back at the pool area. One of the barmaids was removing the plastic covers from the bar's beer taps, in preparation for the forenoon opening. He would return later, after a couple of beers at, *Hole in One*. No food there today. That was for Sunday. Mid-afternoon, he'd have a beer back at the pool, enjoy some sun, then head back to his balcony for some more sun, wine, olives and pistachios. He took the lift down to Reception, looked in a large mirror framed in ornate brass, adjusted his sunglasses and gave his fedora a slight tilt to the left. The pleasant young lady on Reception smiled warmly, as he passed and made his way outside.

It was a short, but a very pleasant stroll along this stretch of Estrada Monumental, past the small taxi rank, sheltered by a wall of hanging, sky blue tiny flowers, beneath which the two or three waiting drivers sat on tree stumps, chatted and smoked their cigarettes. Now he had reached the small banana plantation. As always, James stopped, looked up and studied the trees. *How different from the fruit sections at the supermarkets back home, to see the bananas grow 'in situ',* he thought.

Some distant, dark clouds hung over the Atlantic as he entered, *Hole in One*. His umbrella might be needed on the way back. He walked through the bar and headed out onto the terrace. A few couples were enjoying their drinks and club sandwiches. His preferred table was free and handy for the large, mechanical canopy, should there be rainfall. A complimentary bowl of crisps arrived with his beer. The handsome, tall young waiter smiled generously. He had been on duty the night before and had keenly watched James and his partner perform their salsa as he waited at the bar for a drinks order.

"Where did you learn to dance like that?" he asked politely.

"Oh, it was a long time ago, back home," James replied.

"I would like to dance like that." The young man had the slender, well-formed figure befitting a male dancer. James thought he'd look good on the dance floor.

"Maybe the lady will ask you to dance with her one night. She will teach you." The young man blushed.

"She dances only on her own, or with her husband."

"Or with me," said James, with a wicked smile.

Ominously dark clouds were approaching this side of the island. An air of chill began to pervade the terrace. Quickly, two waiters went over to the canopy mechanism, started turning a handle each and soon the area was prepared. Customers pulled their chairs in more closely to their tables and those without shelter moved under the terrace canopy or inside the bar. James was well protected. He nibbled a crisp and took a sip of beer. The waiters now methodically but quickly removed cushions from any exposed chairs and stored them inside. They stood on each side of the entrance to the terrace, like guards waiting for something to happen. James heard the first drops of rain patter on the stout green canvas above him. In no time, the terrace was framed in unbelievably heavy rain, with customers safely sheltered under the canopy, hypnotised by the spell and the monotone echo of the subtropical torrent.

Ten minutes later, as he polished off his last crisp, the rain clouds had passed, making way for a vivid blue sky and brilliant sunshine. The pavements outside on the Estrada and the bar's cobbled terrace within soon began to dry, the faint appearance of steam rising into the now-warm air. A waitress took a cloth over the chairs, wiping away any surplus water, before replacing the cushions. The two waiters returned to the canopy, turned the handles and the green canvas was gradually rolled back into its sealed position. Some people picked up their drinks and reclaimed their original tables. James ordered a second beer as the turquoise and white colours and the steel trims of the well-washed static Cadillac now gleamed in the sunshine.

Chapter 22
The Satisfied Artist

On his way back, James called in at the minimarket, to replenish his usual supplies for his apartment. He'd store them away then head up to the Pool Bar for one more cool beer and some sun, before his Speedo sun session on his balcony. Miguel saw him approaching and turned on the Coral tap. The usual, local black and white indifferent cat meandered around the tables by the pool, expecting a morsel or two from any gullible guests, enjoying a bar snack. The animal always gave James a wide berth. He liked cats and they usually liked him. This one, however, was obviously a fussy pussy; no food, no 'miaow' and no friendly brush against your leg, dear.

The sun was approaching the left side of the tall palm tree. James changed chairs and welcomed the fullness of the warmth. He'd head down to his apartment after this beer and strip off for an hour of semi-private sun on his balcony. *Perfect,* he thought to himself. He placed his euros and a tip inside the drinks menu, which Miguel strategically collected as he passed the table, carrying a tray of plates and glasses for the wash. Miguel was a very pleasant, congenial family man, always very efficient, with a reserve of friendly jokes in slightly broken English, which invariably added to the humour. James picked up his shoulder bag, pushed in his chair, thanked Miguel and made for the lift. On his way, he stopped to look down at the gardens below, at the Miramar pool and his apartment above, on the first floor, bathed in resplendent, purple and peach bougainvillaea.

He turned the chair on the left of his balcony to face the sun and draped his pool towel over it. Black baseball cap now in place of his fedora, he wouldn't want to get a sun cream stain on that and black Speedos on, he was guaranteed to top up his near overall tan. He'd sometimes get some morning sun on his back and legs, before going out in the forenoon. Now, he was all set for his front, on his slightly reclining chair, a glass of chilled white wine, a small bowl of pistachios and a small plate of the best, small black olives. Sunglasses on, cap tilted slightly to the left, and apart from an occasional, civilised voice below his balcony, a quiet splash in the pool and the steady upward flow of the small, poolside fountain, it was pleasantly peaceful. *Perfect,* thought James, as he sipped his local, good value Porta da Ravessa white wine, popped an olive in his mouth, and then cracked open a pistachio.

After a few minutes, he could feel his skin respond to the welcome warmth of the sun, his body glowing with carefully applied sun cream. A small gecko briefly appeared farther along the ledge, stopped then scuttled behind the bougainvillaea. On the mosaic table, his travel clock showed four thirty-five. One more hour, then a shave, shower and his evening wardrobe. Casual, but smart tonight, James had decided. And no downhill taxi tonight, he'd walk into town.

At six-thirty, he started his walk towards Avenida Do Infante and down the hill to Avenida Arriaga, passing underneath the jacarandas. No Winter Garden beer this evening, but a Saturday evening stop at *Cafe Apolo,* for one beer, then an espresso and a Constantino brandy.

The cafe was quiet and James had no problem securing his preferred table where his beer soon appeared. He'd enjoy his refreshment, take his time, then have a leisurely stroll along the Promenade, on his way to the Old Town and, *Le Jardin.* "Nice jacket, Mr James," commented Julio, as he laid the espresso and brandy on the table.

"Yes, I like it also, Julio. It's woollen and will keep me warm if it gets colder later." Like his black cotton jacket, James only wore his green woollen jacket on holidays. With his aquamarine Neru shirt, navy trousers, slip-on brown shoes and his navy silk breast pocket hankie, he felt the part for his Saturday evening aperitif at *Cafe Apolo* and his evening meal at, *Le Jardin.* "Take it easy, James," he said to himself. "We have all the time in the world."

He made his way down towards Avenida Do Mar, taking note of the unmarked, occasional narrow steps on the way. He'd often see unsuspecting tourists skip a heartbeat and utter an embarrassed laugh, as they missed the slight change in levels, but nonetheless somehow managed to maintain their balance. James crossed over the avenue and proceeded at a leisurely pace along the Promenade. "All the time in the world," he had said to himself, as he relaxed outside *Cafe Apolo.* Now, as he strolled along the Promenade, looking over to the large, impressively lit cruise ships, with the backdrop of the Atlantic beneath the golden moon, he could hear the silent echoes of Louis Armstrong and, *We Have All the Time in the World.* Wonderful.

He looked up at the houses on the hillsides and the panorama of lights, before turning into Rua D. Carlos 1. He continued along towards the Cable Car Station. A few years before, he'd taken one of the numerous blue cabins from the Old Town up the hill to Monte and the splendid Botanical Gardens. Passengers who take a cable car ride are treated to breath-taking views on the climb and on the descent. On his descent, James had been fortunate to have the cabin to himself, ensuring a fabulous, all-around view of Funchal and the Atlantic beyond. Now, he was walking past the station, closed for the day, its cabins empty and locked at both the Old Town and Monte ends of the ride.

He stopped opposite the restaurant and saw Marcelo, discreetly adjusting the knot of his tie. Crossing the cobbled street, he noticed that both ladies were at their usual table. He gave, the *O Tappassol*, waiters a wave and a smile, then greeted the boys at, *Le Jardin*. His table awaited, with its usual candle, but instead of a small cactus plant, there was a neat little vase of fresh flowers. He gave the ladies a polite wave and took his seat. Luis appeared with his beer and smiled. "Mr James, you are the secret dancer, I think." James gave him a surprised look. A moment later, the penny dropped.

"How did you know?" he asked. Luis placed a forefinger on the side of his nose.

"Funchal is not so big, Mr James. News travels fast." As James discovered later, Luis had a friend at, *O Tappassol*, who, on his evening off had been to, *Hole in One*, and had taken a quick photo on his phone, when James and Ginger were in action on the dance floor. He had shown it to Luis earlier that evening. Luis, of course, had immediately recognised James as the salsa sensation. *Yes indeed,* James thought, *it is most certainly a small world.*

"So, Mr James, you are a man of many parts. There is a lady sometimes here with her husband, who thinks you are a spy. She said so to the two ladies a few days ago. And of course, Mr James, you have also been Dracoola. So, Mr James, who are you really?"

"Oh be quiet, Luis and bring me the menu, I need to get my teeth into something." James mocked a scornful, canine smile, as Luis mocked a look of comic horror.

"Your wish is my command, Mr James," said Luis, with a slight bow, then went inside.

Having thoroughly enjoyed the fresh vegetable soup as a starter, James looked forward to a small main course of fresh, whole sardines, a half lemon, boiled potatoes and green beans. The sardines were bigger than the usual canned variety and four were enough for James, straight from the kitchen grill. He sipped his Versatil. Antonio, wearing a protective apron, was preparing the restaurant's specialist flambe crepes nearby. James could feel the heat from the flames on the back of his neck. As always, diners were focused on the outdoor spectacle. The recipients of the desserts, which were ladled with spoonfuls of berries, hot syrup and the option of fresh pouring cream, drooled as they were laid in front of them.

James turned to face Antonio. "Are you working tomorrow, Antonio?"

"Yes, Mr James, but Monday is my day off."

"Okay, Antonio, I am not here next weekend, so Stroganoff tomorrow?"

"Of course, Mr James, no problem." James knew that the Head Chef ordered the best fresh ingredients for all dishes on the menu, including the butcher meat. The beef for the Stroganoff was always fresh, lean and succulent when cooked. Antonio took the crepe cooking utensils inside. "Never a problem for you, Mr James."

His artist friend Rui had been working inside, but now appeared on the terrace. "Good evening, Mr James." He topped up James' wine glass. "Ready for the sardines?" James nodded. Rui called inside for the order, then discreetly took his phone from his trouser pocket. "I have my gallery with me." He smiled cheekily. For his sins, James usually looked at Luis' gallery of art and would choose an item, which took his fancy. Rui was a well-known local artist, specialising in local scenes, landscapes and portraits. From photographs he had taken outside the restaurant a couple of years before, he had drawn a large charcoal portrait of James, dressed in his glad rags and bowtie. It had been Rui's idea. James had been so impressed by the portrait and had promised to buy it on condition that Rui rolled it up safely in a cardboard tube for storing in James' suitcase, which he did. Since then, there were several other smaller pictures, all framed and hanging alongside his much-admired portrait, in James' lounge. "It is not so busy inside," said the artist. "I can show you my gallery now if you want to choose something." James de-boned the first sardine, squeezed the half lemon over it and took a forkful of the tender fish. Rui slowly scrolled through his art gallery on his phone. James took a sip of wine.

"Scroll it back," he asked. "No, go on." James cut up a potato and forked it with some green beans. He swallowed his food and sipped his wine. "Stop, no, go back," he said. James looked at the picture. "Is this charcoal?"

"Yes, Mr James, and as you know, I always spray it for protection." Rui smiled hopefully and professionally.

"And it's the Old Town" – James observed – "just across from here." The drawing showed the continuation of the street, the entrance to the previous old fishermen's village, now home to small restaurants and local craft shops. The scene was framed in trees, the cobbled street and an old lamppost, almost the height of the picture, to the foreground's right. James studied it.

"What size is it?" he asked. Rui took his phone and looked at the picture.

"Fifty by thirty centimetres."

"Okay," said James, "I love it. Let me see it again." It was a wonderful picture, full of detail in the few included buildings, the foliage, the cobbles on the street and the prominent lamppost, on Rua D. Carlos 1.

"Special price for you, Mr James. I shall bring it on Monday."

"Cardboard tube?" asked James.

"Of course," replied Rui, with his artist's professional smile.

As he enjoyed his Macieira, James contemplated his purchase. It was indeed a lovely charcoal drawing, another original for his lounge at home. On Monday, he would be invited inside to transact the deal, in a quiet corner, away from public view. The usual procedure. One very happy customer and one very satisfied artist.

Chapter 23
Being Happy

The female vocalist smiled at him, as he made his way to the bar. The Head Barman poured him a beer. James thanked him, took a sip and turned to look at the action. Dancers were enjoying the music, a Portuguese foot tapper. He could feel the rhythm start in his heels and toes, the gentle vibration tingling into his legs.

There was no sign of her. And then he remembered the morning flight to Lisbon. *No Ginger tonight, James. And no Navy Blazer.* He placed his beer on the bar, sat on a stool and relaxed. "Take it easy, James," he said to himself. "Give Fred a break." He smiled discreetly. The band stopped for a short interlude. He turned back and saw his reflection in the large mirror behind the bar. "God James, you do look handsome," he said quietly, trying to convince himself.

Tomorrow would be Sunday. A day of rest. Taking it easy sun: morning sun on the balcony; lunch and sun here at, *Hole in One*; back to base and Pool Bar sun; late afternoon balcony sun. Why not? After all, it is called Sunday.

The band infused the air with the first notes of, *Happy*. Again, the floor buzzed with the infectious beat and rhythm, which the dancers responded to with undoubted enthusiasm.

A voice inside him said, *Go on, James, be a devil.* He laid down his beer on the bar, placed his beermat on top, winked at the Head Barman, turned, moved and then mingled with the dancers. "Let's live for the moment," he said quietly to himself.

His feet now tapped freely, his arms swung in time and his hips swayed to the music and the sound of Pharrell Williams' easy, rhythmic voice. The small space beside him was now occupied by two attractive young ladies, who seemed very happy joining James in the free spirit of the dance.

When the music stopped and the applause settled, he thought it better to reclaim his beer. He thanked the two young ladies and returned to the bar, but not before he thought he overheard one of them say to the other, "Great mover for his age, Lucy, and did you see him last night?"

"Yeah," said the other.

"Actually, Tracey, I quite like older men like him." The buzz from his appearance on the dance floor was now fading as he sipped his beer, thinking that Ginger was much more his type anyway, dears.

The Head Barman gave him a big smile. "One more beer?" James nodded and also smiled. "And a Macieira?" Again, James nodded and smiled. At the end of the bar, the handsome young waiter from the early afternoon shift was back on duty, filling a tray with a drinks order. He looked over to James, smiled and cheekily wiggled his body in a dancer's movement. "Keep practising, sonny boy, I'm a hard act to follow," James said to himself, returning a cheekily admiring smile as he swirled the Macieira around his mouth, before slowly swallowing the amber liquid. A man of many parts,

Luis had said. But, as a solo thespian in the play of life, James was quite happy.

Chapter 24
An Easy Day

As he had planned, Sunday was indeed an easy day. He'd taken some morning sun on his balcony, some lunchtime sun on the terrace at, *Hole in One*, Pool Bar sun back at base and late afternoon sun back on his balcony, all well-protected with sun cream, of course. Having looked out his clothes for the evening, shaved, showered, applied body deodorant and aftershave, he had admired himself in the full-length wardrobe mirror, before slipping on his white briefs, which further emphasised his tan. Four more days to keep topping it up. Black leather blouson jacket, white T-shirt, black chinos and black shoes, comprised tonight's look. "Casual, but cool, James," he said to himself as he locked his apartment, made for the lift, ordered his taxi at Reception and headed up to the Winter Garden for a pre-evening beer, before heading into the Old Town.

As always, the flames from the pan had leapt up to the moon and the stars, or so it seemed to James. Antonio was an expert at the culinary, and theatrical effects when making Beef Stroganoff. But never extravagant personal gestures, it was serious, professional concentration for the best results. And of course, James had savoured every forkful of the succulent beef, the sauce, with the tenderest fresh asparagus and a crescent moon of perfectly boiled white rice.

"No more food tonight, Marcelo," he said to the manager, who removed his well-cleared plate. "Only an espresso and a Macieira, thank you. I'm very satisfied and it was very warm today."

"Of course, Mr James," said Marcelo, giving James an admiring look. "I see you have been taking the sun. You look like a young man, very handsome."

"Marcelo, you are a flatterer." The manager squeezed James' shoulder and went inside. James felt good. The late evening air was pleasantly warm. He sipped the last of his wine, as the Porto Santo ferry quietly slipped from the bay, into the port's entrance and made its way to its moorings beyond the cruise ships.

It had indeed been an easy day. He finished off his coffee and brandy. Luis appeared with the bottle of Macieira and poured a generous complimentary measure. "I shall sleep well tonight, Luis. No secret dancing tonight." He toasted the young waiter with his glass, put on his blouson jacket and paid his bill, as the taxi approached. Marcelo and Luis waved as the yellow car drove off. "How is the special project going, Luis?" the manager asked.

"It will be ready before Mr James' last night on Thursday. Maybe in time for Wednesday." They looked at each other and smiled warmly. Marcelo put his arm around Luis' shoulder as they both went inside, *Le Jardin*.

Chapter 25
Missions Accomplished

Monday morning saw James take a leisurely stroll down the hill. There was a slight breeze, so he'd tied his lightweight jersey around his shoulders and made sure his fedora was well secured on his head when walking over the bridge towards Avenida Do Infante. The aquamarine jersey was a fitting contrast to his navy T-shirt, navy dress shorts and his blue-flecked hat. Of course, his faithful, sturdy sandals were well used to his frequent daytime walks in and around Funchal. James was always well prepared for any change in the weather. His shoulder bag not only held his 'Diplomat' umbrella but also a bottle of sun cream. He'd have a beer at the outdoor, *Promenade Bar*, of Hotel Porto Santa Maria, and perhaps a little sun at the same time. His first mission would be a black Americano coffee, a custard tart and a Macieira at, the *Golden Gate Restaurant*, beyond, *Cafe Ritz*, on the stretch of the avenue before, *Cafe Apolo*, and Se Cathedral. With luck, he'd get a balcony table on the first floor. He walked past the pavement tables, greeted the young waitress, as he entered and made for the stairs. The upper restaurant was almost full with morning coffee customers. The louvre doors were open to the narrow outdoor terrace, which held four small tables. James politely walked over and hovered within sight of each. To his dismay, all were occupied. But, wait James–the single, attractive blonde lady at the corner table is looking in her compact mirror and applying cherry-red lipstick. A crumpled paper napkin lay on her crumb-covered tea plate and as he slightly craned his neck, James could see that her coffee cup was drained empty. He stood outside discreetly, giving his fedora a slight tilt to the left. The lady picked up her expensive-looking leather handbag, took out her phone, spoke briefly in French and made to leave. Ever the gentleman, James held out her chair for her. She looked up and down at him. "Merci beaucoup, monsieur." She smiled.

"Ma plaisir, madame," said James politely. "Enchante," he added with a broad smile. She straightened the skirt of her smart red suit, showed James a studied 'up and down' smile again, and made her way inside. James couldn't help but notice her slender legs and her matching, toeless red stilettos, adorned with small, sparkling diamante stones and tiny gold bows.

He'd asked for a strong black coffee. James was a strong coffee man, and it washed down the small spoonfuls of custard tart perfectly. Having finished eating, he wiped his mouth with his napkin and took a sip of brandy. *Even more perfect,* he thought to himself, as he looked over to the imposing bronze statue of Zarco, the discoverer of Madeira, who now surveyed the jacaranda trees along Avenida Arriaga. The imposing Regional Government building stood diagonally opposite, and farther along, facing the avenue, the clock of Se Cathedral shone in the glorious sunlight.

Mission one accomplished. He stopped to briefly look at the Men's window, which displayed elegant leather shoes, interspersed with authentic Panama hats. This was James' classic shop and he would hopefully at some point, produce his credit card and make a purchase one of these days. He passed the shop's entrance and stopped briefly at the Ladies' window, displayed with both casual and elegant shoes, the former decorated with ornate beads, the latter with sparkling stones and tiny ribbons of silver and gold. He wondered was the French lady from, *Golden Gate* a customer?

He walked on and found Pope Paul waving at him again. It was only polite to respond before he passed, *Cafe Apolo*, made his way down to Avenida Do Mar and crossed over to the Promenade. As he strolled at leisure, he stopped and looked left. Above the cafes, the rank of yellow taxis and the occasional palm tree on the avenue, some lucky people occupied established, small apartments with narrow balconies, each one accommodating one small table, two chairs and a direct view of the Atlantic Ocean. Cream-coloured exteriors, dark green paintwork and green louvre doors made for an inviting scene, one which James again stopped to admire.

He continued walking along the adjoining pathways and slowed down between the lush green stretches of grass. He smiled at the hexagonal, two-tone green gelado kiosk, with its ornate roof. The additional, eye-catching feature was the collection of cushioned seats and tables around the kiosk, all in the shape of ice cream cones, with exotic fruits on top. Most of the relaxing customers were 'big kids', no doubt reliving their childhoods, James noted with a smile.

Beyond the end of the Promenade, at the far end of the Old Town, he could see the distinctive, old yellow fort of St James. He had heard it held an excellent restaurant, with views of the spanning steep cliffs rising to the east of Funchal. One day perhaps, he'd give it a shot. For now, he was a paid-up member of, *Le Jardin*. Several feet above his head, one of the continuous cable cars passed over on its approach to the station, its passengers returning from the famous black and white, *Our Lady of Monte church,* and the immaculate public gardens of Monte, at the top of the hill.

Mission two: Before the old fort, stands the more recently built, *Porto Santa Maria Hotel*, an impressive mix of suites, studio apartments, restaurant, bar, indoor and outdoor pools and the outdoor, *Promenade Bar*. James had lived here three years before, on an indulgent autumn break. On his spring breaks, he now made a point of walking along to the end of Funchal's Promenade and stopping here for a beer-or two. As was his wont, he would sit at a table by the circular, natural stonewalled, table height garden feature. He didn't sit too close, not caring for one of the numerous, well-camouflaged geckos to visit his shoulder bag. He applied a little sun cream to his arms, legs and face, taking care to avoid his fedora. He sipped his beer. "This is very civilised, James," he said to himself. A couple were cooling off in the pool. Other couples sat at nearby tables, with or without the shade of a parasol.

A sudden swish of passing wings saw the trained bird fly back and sink its talons into the stout leather-clad arm of the falconer. Standing a few feet away from James, the young man and his bird of prey was a feature for guests to capture on camera or film when the opportunity arose.

The three daytime missions were accomplished. The fourth and final mission would be at, *Le Jardin*, in the evening–not just another lovely meal, but to collect his charcoal picture of the Old Town, a work of art, expertly drawn by his artist friend, Rui Costa.

The ladies were obviously trying to attract his attention as he stepped out of the taxi. He greeted the staff, placed his blouson jacket over the other seat at his table and went over to greet Lesley and Christine with a warm smile and the usual 'moi-moi'. Lesley looked up at him. "It's our last night," she said, with sad, rolling eyes.

"Last night," Christine echoed, taking a sip of her gin and tonic.

"We ate early," said Lesley.

"Packing to do. Early afternoon flight."

"Of course," said James. "Folding up the ball gowns?" Both ladies looked at each other and screamed.

"Oh James, you are awful!"

"But you like me," James said with a broad smile. "Let me replenish your drinks, one for the plane." He caught Rui's eye. "Same again for the ladies, please. On my bill." When he returned to his seat, he toasted them with his beer. A little while later, as they stood up to wrap their cashmere cardigans around their shoulders, Rui, Luis and Marcelo approached the ladies, each, in turn, giving them the customary and gentlemanly farewell 'moi-moi.' It was almost theatrical, and the ladies loved it. As they stopped at the kerb, before crossing the cobbled street to, the *Porto Santa Maria Hotel*, they turned, looked back and smiled in delight, as James stood up and blew them both a respective theatrical kiss.

Having finished his two starter meals; avocado and prawns, followed by melon and Parma ham, washed down with half a bottle of Versatil red, it was time for his espresso and Macieira. Rui passed the table, looking innocently, but expectantly. "And the cardboard tube also please, Rui," said James, smiling warmly at his artist friend.

Inside, in a quiet corner of the restaurant, James carefully unrolled the picture, this part of the Old Town being gradually revealed in front of his eyes: the cobbled street and partial pavement, the foliage of the trees, the restaurants at the entrance to the former fishermen's village, the church steeple, some buildings–one with a small upper terrace, hosting a table with a parasol and two chairs. To the fore, was the old street lamppost. All in varying shades of charcoal and in perfect detail. *Rui is indeed an accomplished artist,* James thought to himself. "It's wonderful, Rui, thank you so much." Rui smiled and seemed somewhat shy as he was politely and discreetly handed a small envelope with payment. He was pleased when James told him how the picture would be framed.

"I know a good shop, where I took your other pictures. This one will look good with a black mount and a mid-grey wooden frame, and glass, of course. It will hang in my main room, for me and all my friends to see." He showed the picture to Luis, Antonio and Marcelo before carefully rolling it up again and placing it back in the cardboard tube. At fifty-by-thirty centimetres and light in weight, this part of Old Town Funchal would fit perfectly in his suitcase.

"Obrigado, Rui." He shook Rui's hand warmly and returned to his table outside. Marcelo reappeared with a bottle of Macieira and poured James a generous, complimentary measure.

"One for the road, Mr James?"

The taxi driver looked across. He'd have time to enjoy a cigarette. James swallowed the last of the amber liquid and reflected on a very satisfying day.

"Missions accomplished, James," he said quietly to himself.

Chapter 26
An Elegant Sufficiency

Below his balcony, the pool glistened in the radiant sun. Kindles and paperbacks were being enjoyed on sun loungers. Easy swim strokes were cutting through turquoise-hued water. An inquisitive gecko scuttled up the wall and out of sight, as James closed the balcony door. He looked around his apartment. All was tidy and in order. One last look in the wardrobe mirror. White T-shirt, not-too tight–*my God, James, look at your tan;* khaki dress shorts, sunglasses, shoulder bag, blue fedora at a slight tilt to the left; sandal straps well-secured for some leisurely walking exercise. A local day today, a walk around the gardens, a saunter down to the Estrada and an easy stroll along to, *Hole in One,* for a couple of alfresco beers. An easy walk back would lead him up to the Pool Bar for a cool Coral, a friendly chat with Miguel, then some mid-afternoon sun, with the optional shade of the large palm tree. To finish, some late afternoon sun on his balcony, with a glass of Porta Da Ravessa chilled white wine, olives and pistachios, would fit the bill perfectly.

Smart casual tonight: black cotton jacket, grey trousers, aquamarine short-sleeved Neru shirt, black brogues and grey silk pocket-handkerchief. "Have a lovely evening, James," he said to himself, with a look of approval in the mirror, before heading out for a downhill walk into town.

A slight, but pleasant early evening breeze sent a ripple of warm air through the jacarandas. Traces of purple-blue blossom were scattered along the black and white mosaic pavements on both avenues leading to the town centre. *I could live here for longer periods,* he thought. *I feel quite at home.* A taxi slowed down to let him cross over.

The pavement tables at, *Cafe Ritz,* were busy, as early evening diners were being serenaded by a trio of accomplished musicians, electric violin, clarinet and keyboard, all in easy jazz harmony. James liked this, turned and quickly sat at an unoccupied table for two. *Live for the moment, James, have a cocktail.* Not really one for cocktails, he would, on a rare occasion sample a Madeiran speciality, aguardente: a strong sugar cane distillation, which could be either firewater or like a smooth aged brandy. To make a cocktail with this formidable base, fresh lemon juice and honey are added to the aguardente, to make a delicious drink, belying its original strength.

"Ola, sir." The waiter was poised with his pad and pen. James looked up and smiled.

"Poncha, por favor." The young man glided smoothly back inside. In the few minutes it took to return with his 'Poncha' cocktail, James had been joined unexpectedly by a slightly familiar, tall, casual but smartly dressed man.

"May I sit here?" the man had asked.

"Of course," James had replied.

"I'm only staying for one drink and the music." He took his first sip of his cocktail. Yes, it most definitely had a kick, he remembered. *A pre-dinner cocktail at 'Cafe Ritz', that'll impress the pals, James.*

The man turned towards the musicians. He looked in his early forties, had well-cut, straight fair hair and wore tortoiseshell-framed glasses. Between sips of white wine, he slightly theatrically smoked a slim cigar. The trio stopped for a short break. The avenue had a steady stream of passers-by, heading for the centre, and most likely, many would proceed beyond to the Old Town, looking for a table at a good restaurant. No problem for James, he was taken care of. Same place, same time, same table. On the way to, *Le Jardin*, he'd stop for an espresso and a Constantino at, *Cafe Apolo*, and watch the early evening go by.

Now he recognised him. He was the man with the distinctive gold crest on his briefcase. The man from the Headquarters of the Regional Government, across the avenue. But no lady this evening. It was seven-fifteen. The elegant strains of the electric violin blended smoothly with the velvet tones of the clarinet and the gentle ripples on the keyboard, creating a perfect alfresco ambience at, *Cafe Ritz*. James finished his 'Poncha', paid the same waiter, gave him a generous tip into his hand, and in turn, received a smiling "Obrigado, sir."

He rose to leave. The man looked up at him. "You are leaving so soon?" he asked, with a slightly feigned disappointed expression.

"Yes, I have a dinner date," James replied, with a confident smile. The man studied James' appearance at length.

"That's a pity, you are an elegant man. I think you would be good company."

"Thank you, you're very kind. Enjoy your evening," said James politely. He pushed in his seat and soon mingled with the passers-by on the avenue. Had he turned back, he would have seen his seat was now occupied by a dark-haired, smooth young man with a well-groomed beard and moustache, gazing lovingly into the eyes of the Regional Government.

"See you for lunch tomorrow, Mr James?" asked Julio, who had just finished his day shift.

"Of course, Julio. Food and wine tomorrow. I shall look forward to that." *In civilian clothes, the hospitality staff always looked completely different,* thought James. Julio was heading across to a narrow lane near the cafe opposite. He was now casually dressed in a red, checked shirt and blue jeans, leaving his white shirt, black trousers and bowtie behind.

James had decided to forego the Promenade this evening. He'd take the familiar, narrow back streets, also leading to the Old Town. Dusk was falling, as he passed busy, small outdoor cafes, serving up food and wine to eager customers. Live music pleasantly pervaded the alleyways, where the flames of candle lamps reflected on well-filled wine glasses.

Luis pulled out his chair. James thanked him and sat down. His beer appeared, Luis looking as enthusiastic as always. "Mr James, we have very nice Beef de Atum a Madeirense, with milho."

"Lovely, Luis, but no starter. Maybe a dessert later." James was partial to a good, fresh tuna steak with Madeira wine sauce and served with deep-fried cornmeal cubes. "And carrots please, Luis."

"Of course, Mr James. Your wish is my command. After the beer, as usual?" With his raised chin and efficient air, Luis went inside with James' order, his own recommendation, of course. A fresh bottle of Versatil was placed on the table and opened by Marcelo, who poured a glass for James.

"Elegant again, Mr James," he remarked with an admiring look.

"Thank you, Marcelo. I always say 'It takes one to know one'."

"Oh, Mr James, you flatter me," said the manager, adjusting his tie knot as he went to capture a couple studying the outside menu.

An elegant sufficiency of compliments tonight, thought James. *First, at 'Cafe Ritz' and now at 'Le Jardin'.* He sipped his wine and looked across to the moonlit ocean beyond. *How perfectly satisfying.*

The evening air was still warm. He took off his jacket and placed it over the chair opposite. No one would be occupying that chair.

After a succulent tuna steak, in a mouth-watering Madeira wine sauce, James had indulged in the excellent Creme Caramel, as always recommended by Rui. Each delicate, smooth spoonful slipped down his gullet with infinite ease. Naturally, it was essential to seal the deal with an espresso and a Macieira, as Rui well knew. "It's my night off tomorrow, Mr James, but I shall see you on Thursday, your last night."

The taxi headed up Avenida Do Infante, onto Estrada Monumental and soon stopped outside, *Hole in One.* He paid the driver, walked through the gate and made his way inside to the bar. A local duo was playing a popular Portuguese song with guitar and keyboard. Tuesdays were quieter nights at the bar but nonetheless attracted a regular clientele. He stood at the bar and watched his beer being poured by the Head

Barman. He had just taken the first sip and laid down his glass when a hand grasped him by the shoulder. "Well, ee' by goom, if it's noot Fred Astaire, the main attraction 'eemself!"

Oh no, James thought. *It's the man from the Gents, again.* "Oh hello," he tried to sound polite. "How are you?" The man beamed at James.

"Joost fine, dandy, in facto!"

A small woman appeared from downstairs. The lady from the Ladies, James surmised. She approached the man. "We 'ave to go, Percy. Taxi's coomin." The man looked at James.

"Ethel's right, ye know. Back to The Lido, to pack oor cases. Time to go time, tomorrow."

"Oh well," said James with a sympathetic smile. "I hope you've had a good time. Bon voyage." James added quietly to himself, "And off you go, dears."

"Ee' it's been loovla," said Percy.

"Aye, loovla," echoed Ethel, as they both made for the exit.

James took a long swig of his beer before answering a call to the Gents. The Head Barman smiled. "You are famous, my friend, after all the dancing." James also smiled and politely disguised a quickstep on his way downstairs.

The blend of Portuguese guitar and keyboard music encouraged James to have a second beer to accompany his nightcap Macieira. It would be straight to bed tonight. Two more whole days to go. *Make the best use of time, James. Live for the moment,* he thought to himself. There were still people out on the terrace and a few tables were occupied inside. He held up the Macieira, swirled it around in the brandy glass, raised it to his nose and breathed in the mellow, honeyed aroma through his nostrils. He sank the last of the brandy, paid his tab, thanked the Head Barman, and disappeared into the darkness of the night.

Chapter 27
Behind Dark Glasses

A light breakfast on his balcony: fresh orange juice, mozzarella cheese, mortadella ham on local seeded bread, a hard-boiled egg, and a strong, black Nescafe coffee. An ideal start to the day.

As a rule, he wasn't an emotional person, but he'd soon be missing all this. However, he'd be back, for sure.

Unbeknown to James, he'd be quite unexpectedly overcome with emotion that very afternoon.

A shower of rain had been forecast. He needed his umbrella on the walk downhill. Although the pavements soon dried in the sun, apart from an occasional lingering puddle, the mosaic stones could be slippery when wet, and pedestrians, especially tourists, took care to walk more slowly. As he looked right, towards the Atlantic Ocean, two large catamarans, in separate locations, were sailing far out, their passengers optimistic about spotting whales and dolphins surface from the depths. To his left, the hillsides were gloriously crowned with two spectacular giant rainbows.

College students were sitting on the steps outside the Escola Cristovao Colombo, named after Christopher Columbus, whose discovery of the New World in the later fifteenth century brought prosperity to the Madeiran economy. The island's strategic location on the highly significant East-West trading route, encouraged ships to anchor, taking on food, and water and assuring Madeira wine as a valuable trading commodity.

And now, as he walked past these young men and women, sipping their coffees from the cafe next door, some enjoying a cigarette, James thought of them as the future of Madeira and its related economy.

On Avenida Arriaga, he briefly stopped to look in the windows at, *Blandy's Wine Lodge.* Nice winestops, but not as classy as his Portuguese crystal. He continued along the avenue, glancing at the window displays in the clothes shops. He crossed over, heading back towards Se Cathedral and, *Cafe Apolo,* opposite. He slowed, as he caught sight of a young beggar, totally limbless, seated on cushions, with his back propped against the wall of an old, traditional building. *Oh God, the poor man,* he thought. James had only a two-euro coin in change. He stopped and placed it in the tin cup. The young man looked up at him. James was not particularly religious, but his instinct led him to say, "God bless you." As he walked on, his mind was full of thoughts: What had happened to him? How does he function? Who brings him and collects him? God help him.

He needed his table at, *Cafe Apolo*, and a beer. He had to think of something else. As he sipped his beer, his mind nonetheless progressed on to the subject of artificial limbs, to the field of prosthetics, and how things had progressed during and since the World Wars, other wars since, and were continually progressing in the present day. Something should be done. *God help him, please,* he thought.

His conversation with Julio made him think of other things. New cruise ships were in port. The cafes and restaurants would be busy. The lunchtime, live music from the jazz guitar, saxophone and keyboard eased his mind. He watched the world go by, and ordered the tomato and onion soup, with a poached egg on top, garlic bread and a half carafe of house red. The last lunch here, for the time being, also warranted finishing off with an espresso and a Constantino brandy. He'd come by for a short while, early tomorrow evening, on his way to, *Le Jardin*, for the last supper.

He enjoyed his food and wine, in the company of, *The Girl from Ipanema*, played beautifully by the trio. Strains of Santana now accompanied his coffee and brandy. He asked for his bill. He was relaxed and enjoying the day. *Take it easy, James,* he thought. *Sunglasses on, a tilt of the fedora, shoulder bag on.* A leisurely stroll along the avenue, up the hill and back to base. That was the plan, but the plan was unexpectedly intercepted.

He turned left, into the small square in front of the cathedral. It was surprisingly empty at that point–hardly a soul around. He turned and looked along Avenida Arriaga, lined with the jacaranda trees. He heard an unexpected voice from behind, a voice from nowhere. There had been nobody there. He turned to be faced by another young beggar with one leg and supporting himself with a crutch. Where had he come from? James was slightly taken aback. He instinctively placed a one-euro coin in the young man's cup. James stood still as the young man turned and slowly limped in the direction of the cathedral. Now, uncannily, the small square was busy with people passing through. He looked up at the clock tower, bathed in sunlight, with its cross gleaming on top.

The experience of meeting the two young men, so soon one after the other, had been profound. Suddenly, and totally unexpectedly as he gazed upwards towards the cathedral, James was overwhelmed by emotion. Behind dark glasses, his eyes filled with tears. With a sharp intake of breath, he turned onto the avenue and faced the blinding sunlight. Tears continued to involuntarily stream down his face as he made his way towards the roundabout and fountain, its rising arcs of water glistening brilliantly in the sun. At a quiet spot, he stopped, took off his sunglasses and wiped his face with his handkerchief. "Oh dear, I hadn't expected that," he said quietly. "That really got to me."

With his sunglasses back on, he was now ready to walk uphill, in the welcome shade of the jacarandas.

His preferred table near the Pool Bar was occupied: the older couple with perennially twinned matching shorts and T-shirts, licking their Magnum ices, slowly yet enthusiastically, as they did after their half pints of lager were finished. James sat on a high stool at the bar and ordered a large Coral. It was busy; sun loungers occupied, no free tables, a few families in the pool and a few people seated on bar stools.

James was a great observer, he knew that. It was wonderfully warm and sunny. He needed a place in the sun; to roll up his shorts, remove his sandals, apply sun cream to exposed parts and relax. Behind his sunglasses, his eyes discreetly focused on the progress of The Magnums, as he'd already named them on previous occasions. In ten minutes, they might have individually licked off most of the chocolate and exposed the remains of the ice cream on the wooden sticks. They were each too 'Magnum concentrated' to speak to each other. James knew they were well organised, in their own way. With his wooden stick licked clean, Mr Magnum waited till Mrs Magnum gradually followed suit, accepted her wooden stick, added it to his, and went over to the bar, to deposit both sticks in the litterbin, along with the two folded paper napkins they had strategically wiped their mouths with. Mrs Magnum gathered up her handbag from the adjoining seat. Mr Magnum re-joined her as she stood up. They pushed in their seats, not a word crossing their lips, headed up robotically to cross the bridge over the pool and presumably return to their Village studio. By then, James was already well established, at his preferred table, with his beer and sun cream at the ready. Miguel came over to wipe away any Magnum traces. "Everything okay, Mr James?"

"Perfect, Miguel. Obrigado."

An hour later, he was back on his balcony, sporting his black baseball cap, sunglasses and black Speedos. A slight recline of the chair on the left welcomed the late afternoon sun. He spread his pool towel over the chair, took off his flip-flops and settled down. To his right, a snack of pistachios and black olives was set by a glass of Porta Da Ravessa on the mosaic table. Although James was very much a red wine man in the evenings, sunny afternoons called for a chilled, dry white wine. He took a sip. Perfect, Portuguese and price-friendly. The cracking open of a pistachio startled a tiny gecko, which darted behind the bougainvillaea. Below, the crescent of sun loungers was almost filled. Some couples were seated on theirs, chatting pleasantly to their friends and neighbours, others cooling off in the kidney-shaped pool. Two young girls played with the spout of the small fountain, dodging the water jets they animatedly aimed at each other. He stood up and looked out to the expanse of the Atlantic.

People walking along the Estrada stopped to look up at Miramar, no doubt admiring the development, with its traditional design and well-landscaped subtropical gardens, *perhaps wondering who the lucky residents were*, James thought.

It was time to shower and change. Casual, but cool tonight: black leather blouson jacket, white T-shirt, black chinos, slip-on casual shoes. *Not unlike John Travolta,* he thought. He admired his tan in the wardrobe mirror, swung the blouson over his right shoulder, locked the apartment door, took the lift down to Reception and ordered his taxi for eight-fifteen. He took the lift up to the Winter Garden Bar, for a cool beer. "A cool beer for a cool cat," he quietly said to himself, with a satisfied smile.

Chapter 28
Luis' Special Project

Last taxi downhill. Tomorrow evening, he'd walk into town and make the last stop at, *Cafe Apolo*.

As they drove along Avenida Do Mar, he could see to the right the lights of the Porto Santo ferry, as it began its approach to the port. To the left, the hillsides, strung with necklaces of lights, never ceased to fill James with wonder.

The driver turned onto the cobbled surface of Rua D. Carlos 1, drove along and stopped outside, *Le Jardin*. Marcelo greeted him as he entered the terrace, smiled and adjusted the knot of his tie. "Good evening, Mr James. Casual tonight, I see. Very nice. Very cool." Placing his blouson jacket over the chair opposite, he took a furtive glance around the other tables, occupied mainly by couples. A small group at two joined-up tables on the other side of the entrance watched in anticipation, as Antonio theatrically prepared the flambe crepes for them.

Luis appeared with his beer. "Your beer, Mr James. Shall I bring the menu?"

"It's okay, Luis. Ask the chef if he'll make me his special asparagus soup. For the main course, I'll have the pork in wine and garlic sauce, with boiled potatoes. Thank you. And of course, the Versatil."

"Of course, Mr James. I shall never forget your wine," said Luis, with a slight emphasis on "never". The young man went inside, with a confident smile on his face.

Antonio served the crepes, much to the delight of the salivating customers. He returned to clean the cooking hob. "It's my last night tomorrow," said James, turning around.

"Are you working?"

"Of course, Mr James. Beef Stroganoff?" Antonio smiled.

"Need you ask, Antonio?" replied James, returning a smile.

"And the avocado and prawns to start?"

"Of course, Antonio. I shall look forward to that. Obrigado."

"A pleasure, Mr James." Antonio went inside with the pan and the cooking utensils.

James overheard favourable comments from the group, who were obviously relishing their flambe desserts. Tomorrow evening, the burst of leaping flames would be for him.

Asparagus soup was not on the menu, but the Head Chef was always willing to make it, especially for James, who savoured it. As he finished his beer, Luis appeared with the soup. "Take care, Mr James, it is very hot." James took a sip of wine and let the soup cool for a few moments, before enjoying it. The Head Chef came out for a breath of air at the roadside. On his return, he looked at James.

"Wonderful asparagus soup," enthused James. The Head Chef smiled contentedly.

"A pleasure, Mr James."

With the asparagus soup starter and succulent pork main course duly consumed with relish, James was savouring another glass of Versatil. The group had left and the restaurant quietly echoed with the social chat of satisfyingly wining and dining couples. Luis appeared at his table, followed by Antonio and Marcelo. Luis held a white carrier bag, with what looked like a long box inside.

"Mr James, it is my night off tomorrow. I shall not see you before you go." He held up the white bag.

"This is for you, a present from *'Le Jardin'*." He handed the bag to James. It was quite heavy. "Open it, Mr James, I think you will like it."

James placed his hands inside the bag and withdrew a long, black box. The three men watched, in anticipation. On closer inspection, James realised with astonishment, that the box was in fact a small coffin, with handsome, brass-like handles on each side, and a hook fastening.

James looked up in disbelief.

"Open it, Mr James," said Luis. James unhooked the clasp, holding the box carefully on his lap. He opened the lid on its hinges. The black coffin was generously lined in blood-red linen. Resting on the red material, lay a large bottle of red wine, with a blood-red top. The label displayed, in a flourish of blood-red script, superimposed with white capital letters: 'DRACULA' and beneath it, a blood-red, winged dragon with a cross in its mouth. Beneath the dragon, were printed the words: 'SYRAH', 'Produced and Bottled by Vampire Vineyards'.

Again, James looked up in astonishment. Couples at nearby tables were looking. "I don't believe this," he said, lifting out the bottle and studying it. On the reverse, he spotted in smaller print, the name 'Nocturno'—as he knew—'made from Syrah grapes, harvested during the night, maintaining their freshness from vineyard to winery.' It was James' 'Wine of the Night' but no longer produced. He looked up at Luis.

"It is the last bottle, Mr James. We kept it, especially for you to take home and enjoy."

"But the label? And, of course, the coffin?" James asked.

Luis smiled radiantly. "I made everything, the coffin, I made by hand, the label on my computer. All for you, Mr James. Like you told me before, you are Dracoola."

Marcelo looked at James. "This is Luis' special project, Mr James. But it is from us all at *Le Jardin*', and as we say in Madeira: 'Presentes Nos Bons Momentos.' You are our best customer and our very good friend."

James could feel a lump in his throat and a tear in his eye. He carefully replaced the bottle and laid the coffin on his table. He stood up and looked at Luis. "Come here, you naughty boy." James warmly hugged Luis.

"Just for you, Dracoola," said Luis, beaming a wide smile. He warmly shook hands with Marcelo and Antonio and thanked all three men.

"This is very special," said James. "Thank you so very much." Luis remained, while the other two went to clear plates and glasses from other tables. Couples were still looking over. "You are a clever and talented young man, Luis."

"Thank you, Mr James. Now, espresso and Macieira?"

"Yes please, Luis. Sim, por favor."

As he was about to close the lid of the coffin, the couple at the next table leaned over and politely inquired, "A special occasion?" James held up the open coffin, with the bottle resting on the red material.

"You could say that with a 'Special Reserve'," he replied, closing the lid and securing the hooked clasp on his 'Wine of the Night'.

At the wooden table across the road, in the darkness, the card players concentrated on their late game. Catman fed his feral friends, concealed in the bushes. The silhouettes of the usual tramp and his dog wended their way towards the Promenade. As he sipped his coffee, he saw the golden moon reflected on the Atlantic, as a large cruise ship slowly sailed out towards the far horizon.

Luis came out with the bottle and topped up James' Macieira. He was wearing a leather jacket. "I am finished now, Mr James. I have to go home." James stood up and shook the young man's hand.

"See you next time, Luis. Many thanks again." Luis looked intently at him.

"I shall get your taxi. Mr James." He signalled across to the driver of the traditional, yellow Mercedes and went inside with the bottle. The taxi drove to the end of the road, returned and stopped outside, *Le Jardin*. Luis appeared and looked at James. "October, Mr James?"

"That's the plan, Luis," James replied.

"We shall not forget the moving chair for the stairs, Mr James." Luis smiled cheekily. James smiled warmly, as the young man left, turning into the neighbouring network of Old Town Funchal.

He stored the coffin safely in the wardrobe, locked his apartment and took the lift down to Reception. Tomorrow would be his last full day, so a walk along to, *Hole in One*, was now on the cards. A couple of beers, some live music and a nightcap Macieira would end a perfect day.

He turned into the Estrada and after a ten-minute walk, he was standing at the bar with a large Coral. It was after midnight. The male vocalist and the band were enjoying a short break and some refreshment. The young, would-be male dancer was gliding towards the bar with a tray full of empty glasses. As he emptied it, glass by glass, he spotted James and smiled. James lifted his glass and returned a smile. This personable young man reminded him of his own youth. *Never mind, James, you're still young and cool, according to Marcelo.*

He took off his blouson jacket and placed it over the stool beside him. In the large mirror, he secretly admired his tan, emphasised by his not-too tight white T-shirt. One more day of Pool Bar sun and sun on the balcony. "James, we are still living for the moment," he said to himself.

He sipped his beer as the band played a Portuguese ballad. Couples danced closely to the sultry rhythm, as the singer brought intense feeling to the words of the song. *It was almost like being in a nightclub,* James thought, briefly closing his eyes. *Where was Ginger now? Would she be here with Navy Blazer on Friday? And Fred? He would be the one catching a plane on this occasion.*

He'd have a light lunch here tomorrow, maybe a chicken sandwich and crisps, washed down with a couple of beers.

The Head Barman looked at him, holding a fresh glass under the beer tap. "Por favor," James said with a smile.

"Macieira?" the Head Barman asked.

"Por favor," James repeated.

"Your Portuguese language is improving, my friend," said the Head Barman.

"Obrigado," said James. "Yes, my friend, how to say 'please' and 'thank you' are essential words–always."

The beer and the brandy were placed on beer mats in front of him. James looked at the Head Barman, with a smile. "A conta, por favor," he said, asking for his bill. With feigned astonishment, the Head Barman looked at James.

"My God, you also know how to ask for the bill in Portuguese? You are a quick learner, my friend! How many years have you come here now? I am impressed."

"Obrigado," said James. They both laughed, turning their eyes to a patiently waiting customer, who smiled politely.

"A pint of Guinness and a Poncha cocktail, please," he asked.

The Head Barman lifted his arms and made a sweeping gesture around the premises. "You see, my friends," he said aloud to the watching customers, "*'Hole in One'* is an international, cosmopolitan establishment. There is only one *'Hole in One'*." The receptive customers cheered enthusiastically in agreement and the three men laughed simultaneously.

Chapter 29
Perfect Plans

James' 'stay local' plan, apart from the evening: breakfast on his balcony; some more sun on his back; casual day clothes and a stroll around the gardens; light lunch and a couple of beers at, the *Hole in One*, terrace; a couple of beers and some sun by the Pool Bar; a snack, a glass of white wine and a little late afternoon sun on his balcony; shower, shave and dress for his last evening; a stroll down the hill, a stop at, *Cafe Apolo,* for an espresso and a Constantino, before heading on for his last supper at, *Le Jardin*. "Sounds like a good plan, James," he said quietly to himself. He was well experienced at making plans–both socially and professionally.

Back at base, he had thankfully secured his preferred table by the Pool Bar, fedora at a slight tilt to the left, sunglasses on, sandals off, some sun cream applied to exposed areas, and a cool Coral served by the ever-attentive Miguel.

And then they appeared, having robotically walked over the pool bridge, the Magnums–predictably dressed in their twinned, matching T-shirts and shorts, pretending not to look at his table. He deliberately studied the grandeur of the large palm tree, from top to bottom, then slowly took a sip of his beer, with relish. "This table is well and truly taken," he said to himself. "Off you go, dears."

After a second indulgent beer, it was time for the last, late afternoon sun on his balcony. He left his tab and a tip on the drinks menu on the table, shook hands with Miguel, walked along the terrace, and looked down at the lower pool, gardens and his bougainvillaea balcony. In the background, terracotta roofs on the hillsides above were resplendent in the late afternoon sun.

Having soaked up the last of his late afternoon sun, cracked open the last pistachio, popped the last black olive in his mouth and drained the last of the Porta Da Ravessa white wine from his glass, it was time to shower, shave and dress for the evening. After breakfast, he'd already arranged his clothes for packing on the spare bed. He'd have to pack strategically, in order to accommodate his small purchases from the Mercado, the cardboard tube with the Old Town rolled up inside and, of course, the coffin. No doubt there would be an excess weight charge for that, but it would be well worth it for such a unique item.

His green woollen jacket, navy trousers, aquamarine Neru shirt, brown brogues and navy silk handkerchief, all combined to make for a well-coordinated outfit for his last evening in Funchal.

As he turned left on the Estrada, the warm evening air brushed his face and wafted a whiff of aftershave into his nostrils. *Oh dear, James,* he thought to himself. *I think we may have overdone the Chanel.*

The last evening walk down both avenues saw him pass once more under the jacaranda trees. He had smiled when

Julio had pointed to the flower petals on his fedora when lunching at, *Cafe Apolo*.

On Avenida Arriaga, opposite, *Cafe Ritz*, he looked down and spotted a perfect whole flower on the black and white mosaic pavement. He picked it up and admired its purple-blue beauty. He looked at his reflection in the mirrored glass of the bank building and carefully threaded the fragile blossom through his buttonhole. It was the ultimate touch of class to his evening outfit. Absolutely perfect.

James looked back at the trees, which were bathed in purple-blue. He turned to the mirrored glass and once more admired his reflection, as he gently touched the flower on his lapel. People passing by may well have overheard him say softly aloud, "Jacaranda, Mr James."

"How chic, James," he said quietly to himself. "You think of everything."

Having passed, *The Golden Gate*, he looked across to the Regional Government Headquarters and smiled, thinking of the smart man with the tortoiseshell-framed glasses. Before turning into, *Cafe Apolo*, he waved back to Pope Paul. It was early evening and the restaurant was quiet. Julio appeared outside, as James sat at his usual table, signing for a coffee with his joined forefinger and thumb, holding an invisible cup. Julio knew that the espresso was synonymous with a Constantino brandy and appeared with both, a few moments later. Placing them on the table, he smiled and looked at the lapel of James' jacket. "Jacaranda, Mr James. You are an elegant ambassador for Funchal."

"You flatter me, Julio. I shall come here again." They both smiled. James sipped his espresso and admired the warm glow of the candle flame reflected on his glass of Constantino.

A loud horn sounded at the departure of the large, *Aida cruise ship*, its distinctive giant eye gracing the bow of the ship. The promenade deck was lined with hundreds of passengers, bidding a fond farewell to Funchal, no doubt one of the visual highlights of their cruise itinerary. Outside the cafes, the slow stream of passers-by watched in wonder, as the huge vessel gradually made its way from the port to the bay, leaving Madeira behind and heading towards the Atlantic Ocean beyond.

It was eight o'clock. He swallowed the last of his Constantino. Dusk was approaching and lights were being illuminated in the narrow streets and in the alleyways, and on the hillsides above. James paid and shook hands warmly with Julio. "Back in October, Mr James?"

"That's the plan, Julio. That's the plan."

He walked past the cathedral and through narrow side streets, passing outdoor cafes with candlelit tables. He crossed over to the Mercado and on into the Old Town. If it's Friday, it's Mercado day. *Tomorrow is Friday, but no Mercado for you, James. There's a plane to catch.*

He turned into Rua D. Carlos 1 and walked along the uneven pavements, past waiters always inviting him into their restaurants. And, as always, he politely declined and continued on to his destination, *Le Jardin*.

Rui greeted him and warmly shook his hand. James' beer was already on the table. He took a sip and looked up at Rui. "The cardboard tube is safely in my suitcase. I shall look forward to seeing your picture framed and hanging in my house. As usual, I'll send you a photo from the 'Rui Costa Gallery' in Scotland."

"Thank you, Mr James." The artist smiled and went back inside.

Both restaurants were busy. He saw Antonio appear from, *O Tappassol*, and walk back to, *Le Jardin*. "Good evening, Mr James. I have your beef in the chill cabinet, waiting just for you," he said with a friendly smile. "But first, the avocado and prawns?"

"Yes, thank you, Antonio. It's the last supper too soon." James was cheered by the reappearance of Rui, with the half bottle of Versatil from the evening before. *Come on, James. We are living for the moment. You'll be back,* he thought to himself.

Again, he enjoyed the best, local avocado, not a blemish on the succulent, smooth green flesh, crowned with tender prawns. As usual, he shelled the single prawn last and ate it with his fingers. "How decadent, James," he said to himself quietly as he sociably raised his glass of wine to the young couple at the next table. They were both blonde, well-tanned, obviously savouring the fried espada fish with banana, and washing it down with white wine. The young man turned to James. "Where are you from?" he asked.

"I'm from Edinburgh, Scotland. And you?"

"We are from Gothenburg, Sweden," the young woman replied. "This is our first time in Madeira. It's very beautiful. Have you been here before?"

"Oh yes," said James with a polite smile. "Many times and this is my favourite restaurant. It's the best. Now, enjoy your meal. Bon appetit."

Antonio had appeared, aproned, and holding the small, steel dish with the small slivers of fresh beef. "Two-thirds of that, please, Antonio."

"Asparagus and rice, Mr James?"

"The usual procedure, thank you, Antonio."

"Of course, Mr James, especially for you."

As the flames leapt up to the moon and the stars, the Swedish couple looked startled, but soon smiled at each other and at James. "I can highly recommend the Beef Stroganoff," he said to them. "Antonio is a real expert."

Having said that, James could still feel the heat on the back of his neck, where the first flush of flames had come just a little too close. He removed his jacket and placed it over the seat opposite.

He broke open the crescent moon of white rice, added some of the beef mixture onto his fork and placed it in his mouth. Just perfect. He dissected the eight green shoots of the tenderest asparagus and slowly savoured each one between forkfuls of Stroganoff and rice. Antonio interrupted cleaning the cooking hob and came over. "Perfect, as always, Antonio. Just perfect."

"Thank you, Mr James."" He smiled modestly.

Rui poured the last of the Versatil. "Dessert tonight, Mr James?"

"No thank you, Rui. Espresso and a Macieira will be plenty. The meal was wonderful. As we say, 'a perfect sufficiency'." Rui nodded and smiled. Just as James wondered where Marcelo was, he appeared from, *O Tappassol*, crossed over to the grass area, lit a cigarette and held a conversation with one of the waiters. Rui appeared with the espresso and poured a Macieira into James' brandy glass. James looked up at him. "Rui, I need some light in my life." He smiled, pointing to the finished, small candle.

"Of course, Mr James." The Swedish couple had left, and Rui transferred their candle to James' table. Marcelo crossed over to, *Le Jardin*, and approached James, gently squeezing his shoulder.

"Last night, Mr James," he said with a genuinely sad expression on his face and went inside.

James sipped his Macieira. This was his favourite brandy. As usual, he'd buy a bottle at duty-free, before the flight. He sipped his espresso and looked across the road. The card players were privately focused on their game at the rustic wooden table. Catman was leaving his feral friends to enjoy their alfresco dinner in the privacy of the bushes. Having finished their complimentary food beneath the large tree, James watched the usual tramp and his faithful dog shuffle their way towards the Promenade until their dark silhouettes were outlined beneath the light of the moon.

It was like watching a scene from a play, again and yet again, with the same cast of characters and the same finale, James thought. It was almost theatrical, and he had the best seat in the house.

The quiet strains of an orchestra softly echoed from inside and reached James' ears. After a few seconds, he recognised the instrumental music and knew it was playing especially for him. *Now James, don't get all silly and sentimental,* he thought to himself, with a sudden lump in his throat. Marcelo appeared with the bottle of Macieira and poured a generous measure. The music was most appropriate. Marcelo looked at him. "Time to say goodbye, Mr James."

"Marcelo, you think of everything. I am not crying, it must be the aroma of the Macieira in my eyes," James lied as he wiped a slow tear from his left eye. He was not an emotional person. James thought positively. He'd be back in October. The usual procedure, as always. The klaxon of the vintage car sounded as it passed the restaurant, bounced over the cobbles, slowed down and drove through the gates of, *Hotel Porto Santa Maria*, dropping off two passengers.

James smiled at the fun of it.

The yellow taxi reversed slowly, drove to the end of the road, turned at the entrance to the Fisherman's Village, returned and parked in front of, *Le Jardin*. Marcelo held out James' green woollen jacket and helped him slip it on. James shook hands with Marcelo, Antonio and Rui. "See you in October, Mr James?"

"Of course, boys. That's the plan. Same time, same place, same table. I'll send you the usual postcard, with my dates." As he opened the door of the Mercedes, to sit beside the young driver, he looked back to see his friends from, *O Tappassol* and *Le Jardin*, wave in unison as the car drove off along the cobbles of Rua D. Carlos 1, towards the town centre, onwards and upwards.

The driver turned briefly to look at him. "*Hole in One*?"

"Por favor." James smiled.

His flight would be at two o'clock. The airport transfer at ten o'clock. He'd organised all items for packing, it wouldn't take long when he got back to base shortly. *Live for the moment, James: one more beer and a nightcap Macieira.* Set your travel alarm. No breakfast–just a strong, black coffee on his balcony.

Hole in One, was busy. Regulars and holidaymakers enjoyed an early start to the weekend on Thursdays. Although, James noticed the usual Friday male vocalist was on stage tonight with his band. Couples and female friends took to the floor when he announced that the next song would be John Paul Young's-*Love is in the Air*. James knew his feet would be tapping as he sipped his beer at the bar. He'd be in the air tomorrow. He furtively looked around the dancing area, and the bar and was somewhat relieved to see no Carmo in the crowd.

James had usually been a bit sceptical of those who advocated ESP: Extra Sensory Perception. But now, out of the blue like an apparition, she appeared from the gathering crowd on the dance floor: the lady in jacaranda blue. James' eyes were once more transfixed on her. As she met his gaze, he turned to look at Navy Blazer, who nodded and swept his hand towards Carmo. And, just as in his dream, she beckoned James with a seductive forefinger, adorned with a large amethyst ring. The band struck up, the vocalist brought the lyrics of, *Love is in the Air,* to life and James and Carmo began their performance; dancing, swinging, revolving, laughing. The others cleared the dance floor for the main attraction. James was in heaven as Carmo's jacaranda skirt revolved and took flight, much to the crowd's delight.

Seated at the bar, Navy Blazer took a sip of his white wine and marvelled at the magic spell his wife had spun on this man and the crowd. She was without question good for his reputation and his business in Madeira.

As the song grew to a close, the dancing couple flourished their closing, coordinated moves, and with James' arm tightly around Carmo's waist, they took their bow. The applause and cheering were deafening. James kissed her on the cheek, to the polite approval of Navy Blazer.

The band saluted them and stopped for a break. James and Carmo walked over to Navy Blazer, whose hand James shook.

They exchanged sincere smiles. "Thank you both," he said warmly, adding as he looked at Navy Blazer, "You have a wonderful wife."

"I know," said Navy Blazer, kissing the back of Carmo's hand.

"I fly home tomorrow, so I must leave you now. Thank you once more for a memorable dancing experience. It was wonderful." James politely bowed to them both and made his way along to his place at the bar. "Order your Macieira now," James said to himself. "No more beer tonight, Fred. Next beer, one at the airport."

The Head Barman placed the Macieira on the bar, aware that James was flying tomorrow. He paid for both drinks. "Back in October, my friend?"

"That's the plan," James replied.

"You bring your dancing shoes with you?" asked the Head Barman, with a broad smile.

"I would hate to disappoint you," said James, with raised eyebrows and an even broader smile. "Some of your customers call me 'the main attraction'." The Head Barman looked over his shoulder. At the end of the bar, the young waiter, the would-be dancer, was placing drinks on a tray. He looked up and smiled at James.

"Not only the customers, my friend. You have an admirer, I know."

James paused and looked at the Head Barman, slightly astonished. "Really? You think so? Surely not." Tapping the side of his nose, the Head Barman moved along the bar to serve another customer. He looked back at James and winked at him with a wicked smile.

The young waiter passed behind James with his tray and laid the drinks on the nearest table. As he turned, he looked at James intently, in the large mirror behind the bar. James turned and looked at the young man. He had to politely dissuade him that his attention would not be reciprocated.

"My name is James. What is your name?"

"My name is Carlos."

"Well, Carlos, I am leaving tomorrow. You are a nice young man, and I wish you well with your future." The young man smiled.

"You inspired me, Mr James. Since I was a young boy, I wanted to become a professional dancer. I finally decided a few days ago. I may never see you again. I leave Madeira after the summer. I have applied for a place at The School of Dance in Lisbon. My parents are very pleased."

James sensed both a pleasant surprise and relief and looked at the would-be dancer.

"In that case, Carlos, I really do wish you all success with your future. I think you will do very well."

He held out his hand and shook Carlos' hand warmly. "Who knows, maybe one day, when you are the main attraction, you will return to Funchal and teach me to dance professionally."

"I would like that very much, Mr James."

They held eye contact and smiled at each other. The Head Barman called for Carlos to attend to customers. "I have to go, Mr James."

"I also have to go, Carlos. Good luck."

James instinctively felt the need to gently, but purposefully squeeze the well-formed shoulder of the young waiter and dancer-to-be, who paused, looked intently at him and said, "Thank you, Mr James," before returning to his duties. James drained the last of his Macieira and placed the empty glass on the bar. Before leaving, he caught the attention of the Head Barman. "I shall see you in October, you naughty man." They shook hands and smiled warmly at each other across the bar.

It was just after midnight. As James turned left onto the pavement of Estrada Monumental for the short walk back to Miramar, the warm air still held the scent of subtropical flowers, and wafted echoes of live music, to set his feet tapping on the tarmac.

All items folded and carefully packed, his suitcase was lying, lid down, on the spare bed. In the morning, he'd add his toilet bag, today's briefs, and lock the case. The coffin took up a fair bit of space and added weight. It was well wrapped in two of James' T-shirts. He draped a pool towel around his shoulders, slid open the balcony door and stepped outside. The sun loungers were neatly stacked away from the pool and on the grass, their cushions folded and stored away.

He scanned the crescent of apartments. A handful had lights on, residents perhaps enjoying a nightcap on their balconies.

The fridge. He'd finished all his breakfast and snack provisions. It was one o'clock. His travel alarm was set for seven-thirty. Airport transfer at ten o'clock. Six hours' sleep was adequate. He went back inside, walked along to the small kitchen, switched on the light and opened the fridge. There was still one item on the lower shelf behind the door. He picked it up and looked at the familiar old gate on the label, with the words 'Porta Da Ravessa'. There was enough white wine for a small glass. James hated waste.

He secured the towel around his shoulders and sat on the chair to the right. The waning moon cast its reflection on the Atlantic. On the far horizon, just visible was the silhouette of a large ship. James sipped his wine and looked up. He wasn't an astronomer, but in the darkest blue sky, he could, without a doubt, make out a distant but clear constellation. He recognised the seven bright stars, in the shape of The Plough and gazed in wonder. *My God, James. How absolutely perfect: an indulgent last nightcap, under the moon and the stars.*

Chapter 30
The Usual Procedure

Dressed in his travel clothes, suitcase and travel bag resting by the door of the apartment, James walked out onto the balcony. The sun loungers were laid out around the pool, some already occupied by the usual residents, ever faithful to their places in the sun. The usual swimmers were swimming from one end of the pool to the other, and back again, performing their pre-breakfast exercise routines. Pleasant people held quiet, pleasant conversations below his balcony. He took one final look at the scene–the pool, the large palms and the subtropical gardens. He gently held some bougainvillaea, watched by a safely concealed gecko. Turning into the apartment, he closed the sliding door and drew the screens.

James stopped to look in the wardrobe mirror. He checked the pockets of his blouson jacket and trousers. He combed his hair straight back, his tanned face emphasising the hint of silver-grey on his temples. He undid the top two buttons of his black Neru shirt, admiring more of his well-nurtured tan. "You handsome devil you," James said aloud to himself, placing his travel bag on his shoulder. He checked the apartment, opened the door, placed his suitcase in the corridor, closed and locked the door and made for the lift.

He handed his key card in at Reception. Ricardo was busily focused on his screen but looked up. "Your car is waiting, Mr James." Outside, beneath the tall palm tree on the small island of subtropical plants and flowers, the rear door of the black saloon was being opened by the driver.

"Thank you, Ricardo. See you in October."

"Of course, Mr James. Enjoy your flight."

He waited for an older couple to go out the entrance door and head for the sloping, cobbled driveway. He wheeled his suitcase down the ramp, handed it to the driver and settled into the rear of the car.

Turning left from Estrada Monumental, they headed uphill, through winding streets and onto the motorway. James briefly looked back at the wondrous panorama of Funchal and the large cruise ship at the port. The view disappeared, as the car entered and drove through hillside tunnels, eventually reaching the final stretch of motorway and the approach to the airport at Santa Cruz.

Three airliners were parked near the terminal building, the short runway awaiting the next arrival or departure. James felt that familiar tingle start to run up and down his spine.

Having completed the formalities of Check-In, Passport Control and Security, he headed for Duty-Free and the essential bottle of Macieira, for his drinks cabinet back home. Now he could relax and have one large Coral beer before the two o'clock flight to Edinburgh.

From his table, he looked out at the hillsides above the airport. Santa Cruz also bore the familiar, but the lesser feature of terracotta roofs, interspersed with the occasional vineyard.

Settled in his usual aisle seat near the front of the plane, James still liked to politely lean over and watch the plane taxi slowly, on its approach to the runway, passing only a few yards from the edge of a sheer drop into the Atlantic. Some passengers covered their eyes, as the aircraft gradually manoeuvred to face the runway. Conversations mellowed. Silence prevailed as the engines revved up, and the plane progressed from an initially slow start to a sudden, thundering acceleration.

People held their breath in awe. James smiled, as the aircraft rose majestically above the void of the Atlantic, immediately below.

He caught sight of the llhas Desertas; the small, narrow deserted islands, inhabited by a few goats, rabbits and large, black, dangerous spiders. *No wonder they were deserted,* James thought, with a slight shiver.

Turning north, he then caught sight of the more inviting island of Porto Santo. Maybe one day, he'd take the ferry over and spend a day near the beach, in the shade of a cafe, with some food and wine. Maybe, but he was too fond of Funchal to leave it for a whole day.

As usual, he ordered two small bottles of the Chilean Merlot, and some cheese snacks, perfectly adequate for the time being. Back home, he'd have his local couple of beers, then later, a lovely Chinese meal at his friend Peter's, *Kwok Brasserie*, with some red wine. He'd look forward to that.

There was no more land below, only the vast expanse of the Atlantic Ocean. The young couple seated next to him was wired into their separate technology, headphones on, focussed on separate screens, not a word of conversation passing between them. *Oh well,* thought James. Besides, he preferred in such circumstances, to remain incognito.

He withdrew his paperback from the seat pocket in front and decided to return to it, after an absence of two weeks. Successfully fulfilling his mission plans had, after all, left little or no time for reading. Unusual for him, he had omitted to take a bookmark. However, the few pages he had read were now marked by the pressed, delicate, dried item he had inserted after his last evening in Funchal.

He opened the book. The trumpet-shaped, purple-blue flower, the size of his buttonhole made for a perfect, small bookmark. He looked at it, touched it gently, smiled and said quietly to himself, "Jacaranda, Mr James."

****